THE CRUISE OF THE
KRONPRINZ WILHELM

The Kronprinz Wilhelm, the "Mystery Cruiser" which made German history in the early days of the World War.

THE CRUISE OF THE
KRONPRINZ
WILHELM

by Count
ALFRED *von* NIEZYCHOWSKI (*Niezy*)

Foreword by REAR-ADMIRAL WALTER McLEAN, U. S. N.

Introduction by
COUNT LUCKNER

ILLUSTRATIONS FROM PHOTOGRAPHS

GARDEN CITY, NEW YORK
DOUBLEDAY, DORAN & COMPANY, INC.
1931

Describing the Experiences and Adventures of an
Officer in the German Naval Reserve during
the Historic 251-day Cruise of
the *Kronprinz Wilhelm*.

FOREWORD

It is with a distinct sense of pleasure that I jot down these few introductory lines to Count Alfred von Niezychowski's story of the adventure of the Kronprinz Wilhelm. *Fate made me one of the first auditors of Count von Niezychowski's dramatic narrative. I was Commandant of the Norfolk Navy Yard when the* Kronprinz Wilhelm *was interned there, as the United States then was not at war with Germany and the* Kronprinz Wilhelm *was a friendly visitor. Count von Niezychowski, the nephew of my friend, Ambassador Baron Hengemüller, became my guest. It was during his brief sojourn with me in Norfolk that I first heard the story of his ship's 251 stormy days on the high seas, pursued by the combined Allied fleet. I then expressed the hope of some day seeing his thrilling narrative in print.*

The entrance of the United States into the World War in April, 1917, two years later, converted the Kronprinz Wilhelm *from a friendly visitor into a prize of war, and Count von Niezychowski and his associates from guests into war prisoners. It did not, however, detract from the romance of the* Kronprinz Wilhelm's *adventure, or from the chivalry of its crew, or from the charm of Count von Niezychowski's narrative.*

To-day, ten years after the World War, this book is something more than the record of an enemy raider. It is a messenger of peace. Count von Niezychowski's narrative, no doubt, will help to remove from the German naval men the

vii

stigma of "pirates" with which some of us, in the heat of war, were inclined to brand them. It shows that Germany, in war, had the same sense of chivalry on which we prided ourselves, and which distinguishes civilized warfare from the fighting of barbarians.

WALTER McLEAN
Rear Admiral (retired) U. S. N.

Annapolis, Maryland
December 27, 1928

TABLE OF CONTENTS

CONTENTS

LIST OF ILLUSTRATIONS

INTRODUCTION

WE HAVE had tales of the exploits and adventures of the men who fought in battleships, of the submarine war with its fights between U-boats and mystery ships, and also of the cruise of my old windjammer. But so far as I know, there is one wartime sea tale that has never been told, the yarn of the steamer that turned commerce raider. Now we have it in this book.

I am glad, too, that the author happens to be a Pole. Count Niezychowski spins his tale in a way that may carry more conviction to non-German peoples than if he were a Prussian or a Bavarian. He writes like the jolly fellow that he is. I met him recently in Detroit, his adopted city. Although he is a Polish nobleman who fought for Germany because he happened to be connected with the German Merchant Marine when hostilities broke out, he is now an American.

The *Kronprinz Wilhelm* steamed back and forth and up and down the Atlantic Ocean throughout most of the first year of the war. Allied vessels of every description were on the lookout for her. How she eluded them during a cruise of nearly forty thousand miles is astounding. By Joe, that wireless man on the *Kronprinz Wilhelm* must have been a wizard second only to Marconi! Count Niezychowski's tale gives us a most interesting picture of life at sea during a hazardous and exciting cruise. That yarn of his about the officer who acted as the ship's oracle by always getting a nose bleed just before each capture is a corker. Then there is the story of how part of their crew rode out that terrific storm just off the coast of Uruguay. But the one I liked best of all was the yarn about the way the sailor stole the cologne from the ship's barber.

By Joe, I am glad this jolly Polish count lived to tell his yarn instead of going down to Davy Jones with his pal Hoffmann.

Count Felix von Luckner

VESSELS CAPTURED AND SUNK
BY THE *KRONPRINZ WILHELM* WITHOUT LOSS OF LIFE TO PASSENGERS OR CREWS

Date	Type	Name	Cargo and Booty	Tonnage	Nationality
1914 Sept. 4	Steamship	Indian Prince	Cocoa, coffee, provisions	2846	British
Oct. 7	Steamship	La Correntina	Meat, coal, provisions, guns, ammunition	8529	British
Oct. 28	Four-mast Bark	Union	Coal, provisions, tobacco, wine	2183	French
Nov. 21	Bark	Anne de Bretagne	Lumber	2063	French
Dec. 4	Steamship	Bellevue	Coal, machine parts, gun metal, two automobiles, oxen, wool, wine, whisky	3814	British
Dec. 4	Steamship	Mont Agel	Six sheep, one pig, one ox, a few provisions	4803	French
Dec. 28	Steamship	Hemisphere	Coal	3486	British
1915 Jan. 10	Steamship	Potaro	A dozen revolvers, important charts, Marconi wireless outfit	4419	British

VESSELS CAPTURED AND SUNK

BY THE *KRONPRINZ WILHELM* WITHOUT LOSS OF LIFE TO PASSENGERS OR CREWS—*Continued*

Date	Type	Name	Cargo and Booty	Tonnage	Nationality
1915 Jan. 14	Steamship	Highland Brae	Coal, provisions, clothing, fresh water, tennis balls, football, pigskins, liquors	7634	British
Jan. 14	Schooner	Wilfred M.	Cod and potatoes	2513	British
Feb. 3	Bark	Semantha	Grain	2280	Norwegian
Feb. 23	Steamship	Guadeloupe	Important documents	6600	French
Mar. 24	Steamship	Tamar	Coffee, provisions, two pigs	3207	British
Mar. 27	Steamship	Coleby	Grain	3824	British
			Total	58,201	

VESSELS CAPTURED AND RELEASED

1914 Aug. 27	Schooner	Pittan	—	—	Russian
1915 Feb. 22	Steamship	Chasehill	Coal	4583	British

THE CRUISE OF THE
KRONPRINZ WILHELM

Chapter I

THE FESTIVAL OF KIEL, 1914

O N THE morning of June 25, 1914, I awoke with a start and looked about me. It was not yet light. I could hear the grumbling of our engines and the tremor of our great ship, the *Victoria Louise,* as she steamed eastward through the waters of the Kattegat; then with a rush the events of the week flashed before me like a gay moving picture.

But a few days before we had been at Brunsbuettel witnessing the Elbe regatta. Our ship, because of its great size and commodious accommodations, had been the grandstand of the fleet. The German Kaiser had come upon our carpeted deck from his yacht, the *Hohenzollern,* and with him were the élite of the land. There was the affable Prince Lichnowsky, German ambassador at London; besides him were Count Pourtalés, ambassador at St. Petersburg; Prince Wedel, commander of Alsace Lorraine; and His Excellence von Dincklage, the intimate friend of my uncle Baron von Hengemueller, with many more. And then the ladies—their gay dresses, their golden hair, their beautiful roses.

That evening the Kaiser had made his great speech. I

can never forget the effect it had. Around me in the spacious dining saloon of the *Victoria Louise* a thousand distinguished faces were turned upon one man. His voice rose over the silence, so that each word fell with the ring of steel. And he ended with the memorable words: "We Germans fear no one on earth, only God." First there was a silence which no movement disturbed; then the applause thundered.

Next day our distinguished guests had gone. The Emperor's yacht, the *Hohenzollern,* was carrying him through the Kaiser Wilhelm Canal to Kiel; while the *Victoria Louise,* which was too tall to pass under the bridges of the canal, was now steaming around Denmark, also for Kiel, to be present at the great annual regatta for which the German harbour had become so famous.

All these remembrances went through my mind as I lay there on my back listening to the engines of the *Victoria Louise* make the ship tremble. Now I stretched my arms, yawned, and leaped from my bunk.

I remember that morning well. The thought that had come to me as I listened to the Kaiser's speech on the Elbe kept recurring to me now. Again and again I tried to forget it, but it would not away.

Dawn was already breaking. As I looked from the cabin bull's-eye, I could see shafts of purple streak the east. Our ship was steaming directly into the dawn. I saw that in a few moments the sun would begin to peep over the horizon. Then I turned to my dressing, shaved, scrubbed my nails—

for some reason I remember all the details—and dusted from the shoulder of my coat some spots of powder which a lady's cheek had left that night of the ball.

Engrossed in these duties, suddenly I heard a call outside. It was the lookout in the crow's nest who had sighted a ship. I went out on deck and up to the bridge. The sun had risen half out of the sea like a great red globe half revealed on the horizon. I looked about for the sighted ship and was beginning to wonder at the dullness of my sight when suddenly in the very heart of the face of the sun I caught sight of a small, dark spot. It was a ship, indeed, and in a minute I could see she was steaming directly west and so upon us.

By this time other officers had come on deck. All gathered on the bridge and stood looking through their glasses at the approaching vessel, wondering of what nationality she could be. Some were chatting, others laughing, still others silently looking at the sea. They, too, were still under the influence of the festivities of the Elbe.

Suddenly one who had his glasses fixed on the sun dropped them and turned half round.

"Men," he said, "it's the *Polarnaya Zviezda.*"

At this a silence fell, while all strained their eyes in the direction. I could feel the pulse of every German on the bridge stand still.

The *Polarnaya Zviezda,* the royal yacht of the Russian Czar—in English, the *Northern Star*—there was a story! The German officers on the bridge held their breath.

Then I heard a muttered oath. The *Northern Star*, as everyone knew, was returning from St. Petersburg with French diplomats who had gone to the northern capital to sign agreements between Russia and France. These, as all Germany believed, related to war with herself. Therefore, the German officers on the bridge of the *Victoria Louise* muttered an oath.

The *Northern Star* steamed swiftly up. She was a beautiful ship. As she came on our port out of the path of the sun, we saw the light sparkle on her copper and glass and snow-white sides. She seemed a floating palace. Not the Kaiser's *Hohenzollern,* not Morgan's *Corsair,* could compare with her. The men on the bridge beside me felt the beauty of the ship. A sailor's eye has a love for sights like this. A beautiful ship is to him like a beautiful being—to be admired—loved. They watched the *Polarnaya Zviezda* till she was out of sight. Then all seemed to start from a kind of trance; they threw back their shoulders, breathed the sea air, and tried to throw off the effect of the *Polarnaya Zviezda* in the thought of the delights to come. For next day we would be at Kiel.

On the morning of the twenty-sixth we steamed past the Kaiser Wilhelm Canal and into the bay. It was the week of the great festival of Kiel, June, 1914. For months all Europe had looked forward to this event. In the spacious harbour of Kiel ships of all nations had congregated— pleasure yachts, passenger ships, battleships. The powerful German navy was there, and with it a large squadron of the

English fleet. Russian, French, Italian, American, Japanese—representatives from all parts of the earth—had assembled in a great semicircle to witness the races for which the German harbour had become so renowned.

The *Victoria Louise* steamed to the centre of the rainbow of ships and cast anchor. Because of her size and commodious dining hall and quarters our ship had been designated the reception ship of the Hamburg-American fleet. From funnel to water line she had been newly painted; and now she lay there on the surface of the bay, decked in the flags, festoons, and streamers of a gala event; while about her on either side in a great bending line lay a thousand ships of all sizes and kinds, festooned like her with patriotic bunting of the respective nations. Music was in the air. It was carried from ship to ship and ran along the mirror of the harbour over the surrounding sea, and the sparkling sun shone down upon a seaman's paradise.

It was Saturday, the twenty-seventh of June. On deck we were rubbing our hands. To-day on our ship the royal reception and ball would take place. Ten launches had been set aside by the Hamburg-American fleet for our vessel alone to bring aboard the Emperor and other guests.

From early morning great crowds could be seen on shore swarming upon the sea wall and wharves. Flags were waving, balloons bobbing, pennants fluttering, colours of every description rustling and weaving in the milling throngs. Cheers and murmurings, intermingled by strains from the bands, rose and fell. At noon we began to note an excited bustle in the crowds. Suddenly the cheering rose to a veritable storm, and a great launch put out from shore. The Emperor was coming!

That night again a memorable ball was held in our dining saloon when the nobility of the various countries greeted the democracy of the others, and amidst music and the dance ladies and lords until late into the summer night initiated themselves into the Kieler Woche.

Sunday morning broke. The sun rose purple and at noon flashed down in splendour upon a happy world. As far as eye could reach—only colour, sparkle, cheer. Our hearts leaped. One night of revelry and now a week of races and delight.

This was at noon, Sunday, June 28, 1914. At that same moment, one thousand miles from our scene of splendour, quite another drama was being acted out. At twelve o'clock on that day in the city of Serajevo the Archduke Ferdinand of Austria and his wife were assassinated. At 1 P. M. the news was telegraphed to the German ambassador to Austria-Hungary, who was on our ship.

We at once signalled for messengers. Two destroyers, one of them the *Alice Roosevelt,* named in honour of the Kaiser's favourite American, came to our side. They took aboard the most important of our guests, then steamed full speed across the bay to the yacht *Meteor,* on which the Emperor was sailing.

When the Kaiser was told the fateful news, his countenance changed, and in a husky voice he commanded the festivities to stop.

Instantly, a great change came over the harbour of Kiel. Commands rang out, abruptly the gayety ceased and mourning began. On the battleships all flags were lowered to half mast. Colours, bunting, regalia, all evidences of joy were hauled down, and in a short space the great harbour took on a most dreary appearance. Now thundered out the first mourning salute. Each of the hundred or more German warships began firing its sixty rounds. Slowly, solemnly, the cannon boomed their deep appeal. Over the bay the smoke spread and settled and daylight began to dim. Between the thunder of the cannon the wail of the bugles faintly lamented from ship to ship. And as of one accord the vessels of all lands began steaming away; while the yachts, which but a few days before had come under such circumstances of happy expectation, were taken in tow and hurried from the scene.

The thousands of cannon salutes paid by the German fleet solemnly ended; silence again fell on the smoky sea. Then our whistles began to signal, the German ships to move, and by next morning not one vestige remained of the great festival of Kiel.

What was now to come?

Of all on board the *Victoria Louise* I was especially fortunate in getting accurate news as to developments. Although I am of Polish descent, my uncle on my mother's side is a hereditary member of the Prussian House of Lords, and another uncle is of the same body. In this troublous hour I was particularly anxious to get news of developments from them, as I believed that international trouble of the first consequence was at hand. I would especially have welcomed a word from my uncle, Baron von Hengemüller, formerly Austro-Hungarian ambassador at Washington, as to the probabilities of war; but, in consideration of my uncertain situation at the time, I did not write to him. As for the diplomats and men of high governmental station on board the *Victoria Louise,* among whom I had numerous friends, these all had left our ship immediately after the murder of the Archduke to take up as fast as possible their responsible posts, so that no counsel from this quarter was forthcoming.

Meanwhile, the *Victoria Louise's* orders were to proceed to Hamburg. We accordingly put to sea, steered north through the Kattegat and Skager-rack, then south again along the Danish Peninsula to the mouth of the Elbe, and so up to Hamburg where we arrived on the third of July.

Here all was bustle and preparation. Ships were coaling frantically. Unnumbered submarines and torpedo boats lay at anchor side by side, getting ready for sea as they awaited eventualities.

I found that many of my friends in Hamburg were sure there would be war, while some were as certain that the matter of the Archduke's murder would be settled amicably. Bets on the outcome were numerous, mostly with the odds on the side of war.

I now got in touch with home. But the news I received was not comforting; only pessimistic predictions, and the counsel to be ready for the worst. I fell into the greatest suspense. At no time from now until the declaration of war did I feel certain which way matters would turn. In this mood I now received my transfer from the liner *Victoria Louise* to the *Prinzessin Irene,* which had orders to make the run to New York.

On the twentieth, after coaling with all speed, the ship dropped down the Elbe and put to sea. As we came through the Strait of Dover, what was our astonishment at finding a great part of the British battle fleet, from largest super-dreadnaught to tiniest of the mosquito craft, in battle array, steam up and decks cleared for action. An ominous feeling came over us. These preparations were not for nothing. Behind the scenes in the various capitals the strings of diplomacy were drawing taut. War was at hand. We were steaming from Europe perhaps to be overtaken by the outbreak of hostilities before we could reach the other side, perhaps never to see our homes again. Under a mantle of cheer we hid our anxiety and when night came prayed for the loved ones we had left behind.

On the twenty-eighth of July we put into Hoboken. Hostilities had been opened between Serbia and Austria-Hungary. But no Great War as yet. Everyone was hopeful. Perhaps things might turn out well after all. I read the New York papers eagerly, but could not gather from them how matters actually stood.

It was now that I wished my uncle, Baron von Henge-müller, were still ambassador to the United States, a post he had held for twenty-five years. Had this been the case I would at once have gotten an understanding of the situation. He was an intimate friend of American presidents, especially of President Roosevelt, as well as of the European heads; had the secret diplomacy of a lifetime at his finger tips, and could have predicted with reasonable accuracy the course of events in Europe during the last weeks of July, 1914. But my uncle had left Washington in 1913.

It was just now that I received my transfer from the *Prinzessin Irene* to the *Kronprinz Wilhelm*. This giant passenger ship of twenty-five thousand tons, which at the time was lying at anchor in Hoboken, had but recently been overhauled and was soon to sail for Bremen with the usual number of passengers. I preferred to be aboard this palatial craft and was counting myself lucky to become an officer in her peaceful service. Little did I dream what she had in store.

The *Kronprinz Wilhelm* now began taking on the usual supply of provisions. Her captain, K. Grahn, showed no sign of what was really going on in his mind. Her officers talked as if they believed the volcano upon which the world was sitting was perhaps not going to blow up after all, when suddenly, like a bolt from heaven, came the declaration of war by Germany against Russia. The die was cast. It was not peace, but war.

Captain Grahn at once received sealed orders from the agent of the North German Lloyd, who in turn had his instructions from the German ambassador at Washington. The *Kronprinz Wilhelm* began to take on huge quantities of meat, general provisions, and coal—far beyond all ordinary needs—while steam was kept up as if for immediate departure. Only a few of the officers knew what these preparations actually meant. Members of the crew shrugged their shoulders, puffed harder at their cigarettes, and stoically reasoned that things must soon begin to happen. Their belief in Germany's invincibility gave them assurance. Some who were curious came and asked me how I thought matters would go. They had heard I was a Pole and, I could see, were wondering how I would act under the predicament of war. Three days later, on the third of August at 8:10 P. M., the command came to weigh anchor.

It was a raw, gusty, drizzly, unpleasant night as eight puffing tugs towed us downstream. Word had by this time been passed around that Germany had declared war on France. Now, then, we were in for it. Outside the harbour we knew there were already enemy warships in wait. We had seen them in the distance. Already we had nailed tarpaulin, mattresses, and paper over windows and bull's-eyes; and in the drizzle of the night we knew we were but a great black hulk, invisible save near at hand. One by one the tugs let go and steamed away. We saw the sparks flying from their smokestacks and watched their lights disappear up the river. A few of us gathered at the rails to take a last look at the blinking lights of New York which came to us through the murky rain. Then the command went down to the engines: "Full speed ahead!" and off we sped, a dark colossus, past the warships in wait for us, into the Atlantic night.

Chapter II

THE "KARLSRUHE" RENDEZVOUS: WE BECOME A MAN-OF-WAR

WHEN the morning broke, I was already up. On the bridge I found my friends, Lieutenants Hoffmann, Brinkmann, and Fix, with other officers, all anxiously searching the horizon for trace of enemy craft. Lieutenant Brinkmann, our wireless expert, reported that during the night he had cut in on calls from London which announced that England and Belgium had declared war on Germany. We thus knew we had to pit our ingenuity against the greatest combination of naval forces ever assembled on the sea.

The two men in the lookout assured us there was no sign of a ship in sight, but even as they spoke the man in the crow's nest megaphoned down that there was smoke in the north. Captain Grahn accordingly altered our course slightly more to the south. It was by all means necessary to avoid meeting the enemy for the present, for we did not have on board a single gun with which to give battle. Thus far ours was only a passenger vessel on her way to Germany, and until further orders it was our single purpose not to be caught.

Captain Grahn had simply been directed to put to sea and await further orders by wireless. These he received soon after we got out of Hoboken, when the S. M. S. *Karlsruhe* sent a message saying that she would meet us on the sixth of August in latitude 25.40 North, longitude 72.37 West. We accordingly put on all speed in that direction. Should we succeed in reaching the cruiser, we would at least have temporary protection against attack, but what orders the war vessel would bring us none could tell.

Lieutenant Hoffmann bet me a box of cigars—he knew I did not smoke and would have to pass them around—that the *Karlsruhe* would take some of our coal and provisions, giving us in return guns and ammunition to fit ourselves out as a commerce destroyer. I agreed with him, but just for the sake of the argument took his bet, maintaining that we would simply provision the *Karlsruhe* and put back into some United States port for the rest of the war. So we shook hands on it and agreed to suspend judgment.

Meantime, Captain Grahn was taking precautions against capture by having the ship camouflaged, a large part of the crew being busy with brush and paint pot repainting the vessel's exterior.

The *Kronprinz Wilhelm,* I should mention, was one of the largest passenger ships afloat and consequently hard to disguise. Her length on the water line was greater than that of two average city blocks, her many decks rising as high above the surface of the sea as a ten-story house. In addition, her four gigantic funnels—so large that the greatest locomotive could have passed through one of them lengthwise without scraping—and the tall masts made her easily recognizable. For eluding capture, therefore, we could not depend so much upon disguise as upon speed; and luckily our twin screws were capable of giving us twenty-five nautical miles an hour, at which rate few vessels could overtake us. Notwithstanding this, we now repainted sides, deck, and bridge a dull sea-gray, giving our funnels a black-banded top. We were soon to learn that this labour was not wasted.

For two days we ran on in a southeasterly course, working diligently at our camouflage while keeping alert for signs of the enemy. Lieutenant Brinkmann constantly warned us when the wireless indicated the nearness of enemy ships. There were enough of them, I can assure you. The sea seemed to be alive all around us. Each hour we picked up news from one cruiser or another and were constantly put to zigzagging in our general direction toward the *Karlsruhe* rendezvous. On our forward mast, about midway to the top, our first lookout station always held an officer and an assistant, while still higher up in the crow's nest a sharp-eyed seaman, especially trained to this service, kept a vigilant scrutiny of the horizon. When the man in the crow's nest discerned smoke or haze which seemed to indicate a ship, he called to the men in the lookout below him; instantly all glasses would be trained in the direction, and the bridge would get ready to act upon the result.

Thus steaming warily onward, we went into the third day

of our cruise—the day on which we were to meet the
Karlsruhe. Morning dawned bright and clear. I came upon
the bridge as usual to take a look at the sea, but nothing
was in sight. Toward nine o'clock, however, when all were
at their tasks, a man in the crow's nest cried suddenly:

"Smoke, three points to starboard!"

We trained our glasses in that direction. Sure enough,
four funnels were rising over the horizon and bearing our
way.

Captain Grahn was on the bridge at the time. In a
twinkling he had descended to the deck and climbed into
the lookout, from which he returned a few minutes later,
having made out the S. M. S. *Karlsruhe.*

Lieutenant Hoffman now came up to me.

"Get ready to hand over the cigars, Niezy," he said. "In
another hour we'll be a German man-o'-war."

The *Karlsruhe,* a neat, shipshape-looking vessel, somewhat smaller than the *Kronprinz,* now steamed up rapidly.
From her trim gray sides jutted the nozzles of numerous
guns, giving her an important, businesslike appearance;
while her four gray funnels, topped with black and belching heavy clouds of smoke, testified to the power of the
engines in her hold. In half an hour she had come up, made
a circuit to starboard, and steamed alongside our port.

Captain Grahn at once went aboard the cruiser and held
a brief parley with her commander. When he returned
after a few minutes, I read the news in his face.

"*Kriegschiff!*" he said. "War vessel!"

COUNT ALFRED VON NIEZYCHOWSKI, *a lieutenant on* *the* KRONPRINZ WILHELM

In a trice the word went round, and the men who had been restless with uncertainty broke their suspense with a hearty cheer. Then silence fell and the first orders went down.

It will be remembered that before we left Hoboken we had taken on board an extra supply of coal and provisions. These we now began transferring as speedily as possible to the decks and hatches of the *Karlsruhe* which was in great need of them.

The cruiser, on the other hand, had on deck two 88 mm. guns, which our derricks now hoisted aboard the *Kronprinz Wilhelm,* together with about fifty rifles and some ammunition.

This work went on with utmost rapidity. There was no minute to lose. The wireless of the *Karlsruhe* as well as our own had picked up a number of messages that morning. There were at least three enemy cruisers not a hundred miles away, and from the conversation passing between them we suspected the presence of half a dozen more within the radius of sixty to seventy miles. We must, therefore, transfer our goods in utmost haste and get away from the neighbourhood.

Meantime, the ship's personnel was to receive an important addition. Captain Grahn, who had so ably commanded the *Kronprinz Wilhelm,* was a man trained to passenger-ship service. Although one of the ablest ship's captains in the service, he could not be called a naval officer, since for such war-time service special naval training is

necessary. Accordingly, Lieutenant Commander Thierfelder now came aboard us from the *Karlsruhe* with fifteen
men of the latter's crew. Henceforth, he was to be our naval
commander, while Captain Grahn should act as his assistant
with the rank of first officer. We, the merchant officers, became automatically full-fledged naval officers, with all their
powers and duties. In this array, I was designated as
"watch officer."

Things now took on a different appearance. The commander's standard was run up and we became a vessel of
war. The men, relieved of the uncertainty of the last few
days and thrilled to become participants in the war, took
on serious, businesslike looks, working with the vigour of
college boys at training. Some of them joked as they
worked, exchanging repartee with the men on the
Karlsruhe. On both decks winches were rumbling, chains
rattling, and booms swinging about. Everything was in a
kind of regulated confusion.

In the midst of this turmoil the lookout of the *Karlsruhe*
suddenly rang his alarm. Instantly the cruiser's gong
sounded and her bugle and drum called, "Clear for action."
Looking up we saw on the horizon the smokestacks of a
large English cruiser.

We were taken completely by surprise. Our extra provisions had not yet all been transferred, and we had not
taken aboard one tenth the necessary supplies of ammunition. But there was no time to lose. We could see at a
glance that the English cruiser, which we soon recognized

as the *Bristol,* a fast ship, had recognized the *Karlsruhe* and was bearing down full speed. We must get away on the instant.

While our cables were being cut and pulled in and the propellers at our stern began to churn the sea, our men tossed over to the decks of the *Karlsruhe* all meat and provisions which were on our deck ready for transfer. This continued until our vessels had drawn too far apart, when what remained was again rushed below decks.

Our band now struck up "Deutschland, Deutschland über Alles," and amidst the repeated cheers of our men, answered by the crew of the *Karlsruhe,* the two ships steamed apart.

The *Karlsruhe* now began making a large semicircle to starboard while we bent off to port, this action of hers being intended to give us time to get away. On seeing this manœuvre the *Bristol,* which had by this time come almost within range, seemed undecided what to do. Recognizing the *Karlsruhe* but doubtful about the *Kronprinz* because of our camouflage, the English cruiser at first seemed to think that we were some Allied vessel in the capture of which the *Karlsruhe* had been surprised. She hesitated, therefore, not knowing which of us to follow, but finally decided on the *Karlsruhe* and gave vigorous chase.

A running battle at once began, clearly visible from our decks. The *Karlsruhe* had brought her long-range starboard guns into play; while the *Bristol,* belching volleys of white smoke and flame, thundered away with her own.

From both ships the white clouds of battle mingled with the black smoke from the funnels, while in the water about them the splashes of sinking projectiles shot up over the horizon. As long as the ships were visible, we could see the orange flash of the guns, but though we used our glasses we could not discern any hits. And the greater speed of the *Karlsruhe* was slowly drawing the two vessels out of range.

When they were finally out of sight of the Britisher, Commander Thierfelder altered our course to the west, steaming ahead full speed. For the moment we were safe, but there was no telling at what instant a new enemy might appear, warned of our whereabouts by the wireless of the *Bristol*.

We were not in the best of moods either. A very material part of our programme had been disturbed. It is true we had now aboard the *Kronprinz Wilhelm* two fair-sized guns with trained crews to man them, but as yet the guns were not in place, and, worst of all, we had taken on dangerously little ammunition.

Our flight had literally been a scramble so precipitate that the *Karlsruhe,* which had previously lowered one of her swift ship's launches, had not stopped to haul it aboard again. We learned later that the abandoned craft drifted to a United States port, where its appearance gave rise to the much-featured report that the *Karlsruhe* had been sunk.

The *Karlsruhe's* wireless, however, informed us shortly after she was out of sight that she had outdistanced the

From the KARLSRUHE *the* KRONPRINZ WILHELM *received a naval commander and equipment for its subsequent career as a war vessel.*

Bristol, but owing to the presence of other enemy craft which, called by the *Bristol,* were steaming up from all directions she could not for the present attempt to meet us again. This meant also that the *Bristol,* no longer in pursuit of the *Karlsruhe,* might now be turning her attention to us.

While our lookouts kept a most vigilant watch and the officers on duty were giving their orders I climbed upon the aft bridge to take a look around and celebrate off-duty by being alone. Over my head the great funnels of the *Kronprinz Wilhelm* were pouring forth vast areas of smoke and sparks, while beneath my feet the ship was trembling under the terrific exertion of her engines, which were driving her almost half a mile a minute. I felt a little dazed by the excitement of the past hour. The first shots of the war seen by us had a strangely sobering effect.

My eyes were on the horizon, but my thoughts were far away at home. So, now the war was on, and I was involved in it. Poland must even now be the theatre of war, and my home perhaps at this very instant in flames. What would become of my people? I thought of my mother. A premonition came over me; I would never see her again. This was destined to be true.

As I stood there sunk in gloomy thoughts, someone tapped me on the shoulder. It was Hoffmann, who had stolen up from behind.

"Cigars, old man," he laughed.

"All right Heinz," I answered, starting from my reverie. "But just wait awhile yet, old man. That cruiser has sent out a wireless to other ships, and if they get in our track maybe neither you nor I will have use for a cigar."

Hoffmann was an optimist.

"We'll get away," he smiled.

But I knew that even if we did get away, the Great War remained; we could not get away from that.

"It looks to me like an all-day chase," was all I could say.

Chapter III

AT THE MERCY OF THE ENEMIES

AN ALL–DAY chase it proved to be. For more than two hours we rushed along in a bee line west at a speed of twenty-five knots. In our hold the stokers were working like demons; while oilers, water tenders, and engineers went rapidly about regulating everything toward the common safety. The life of the ship depended on their efforts. An accident now and all on board would be lost. For Commander Thierfelder had sworn that under no circumstances would he surrender the ship. She would either cruise in victory or go to the bottom bravely, as a warship should. Those who have never been aboard an ocean liner can hardly imagine what it means to maintain a speed of twenty-five knots on such a large vessel.

I went down into the hold that day of the chase to see how things worked under pressure. In the immense fireroom I found everything at a white heat, the great space resembling some oft-seen illustrations of Dante's *Inferno*. In dingy valleys, between tall walls of iron, slaved pigmy men who wore no clothing save a pair of breeches. Their muscular backs, their breasts, their arms and faces, streamed with grimy sweat, so that in the half light friend might not even recognize friend.

These fiendlike toilers worked in pairs, one of which I stopped to watch. One of the two men, shovel in hand, flung open an oblong furnace door. Flash! a very furnace of fiery light shot out, painting the whole neighbouring valley orange. Then the other man stooped, scooped up a shovelful of coal from a pile on the floor and hurled it into the flames, while his sturdy helper held a shovel in front of the man's face to ward off the blazing rays. This process was repeated. Then the same toiler took up a long iron bar—a slicer— thrust it into the depths of the white-hot mass, sliced right and left, and ended by scraping out upon the floor at his feet some white-hot slags.

All this while the sea was heaving the vessel irregularly up and down. The men watched their chance, stoking on the downward plunge of the vessel. Then as the ship rose the slicing bar was deftly withdrawn and the door slammed shut. If not in time a cascade of flaming fire spilled from the furnace upon the floor. But the men were adroit. Usually, they closed the door in time.

Now came an instant's breathing space, after which the two brawny forms reeled down the valley to the next iron door, where the process was repeated.

This same thing was being done all along the line by other couples of toilers. No rest for these men—they must keep up their struggle. The *Kronprinz Wilhelm's* fires must have their coal or the steam will not stay. Four hours of hell, four hours of rest, then four hours of hell again. That was the programme.

In the engine room things were cleaner and cooler, but the complexity of the whole intricate mass of moving steel almost bewildered the eye. To right and left pipes, valves, gears, steel steering arms moving regularly in different directions, pumps thumping like so many drums, steam whirring through invisible valves—all a confused medley of working parts. On greasy steel ladders and gangways the forms of men in overalls dodged in among the moving beams and fly wheels oiling, wiping bearings, turning a valve here, a wheel there, now throwing a lever, again quietly wiping the face of a shaft, or still again perseveringly dodging the strokes of a piston rod to oil between.

I examined the ship's gauges which, because of the terrific speed of the vessel, were registering unusually high pressure. The dials were ranged on one wall like so many clocks, nervous indicators fluctuating as if intelligently over the figures of the cards. Above them at irregular intervals sounded a deep-toned gong which was speech to the engineer. Still lower down stood the engineer's telegraph—a clocklike affair over the face of which moved a pointer hand like the indicator of a pair of scales. This indicator still pointed to "Full speed ahead"!

As I stood there taking everything in, I felt quite depressed. Around me the engines were whirring, the pumps jogging, the gong sounding, the men calling to each other. A fog of steam hung about the place, while the usual oily odour permeated the atmosphere. From overhead beads of water, condensing from escaping steam, dropped down, spattering upon the pipes and floor, while under foot the greasy gangways trembled with the throb of the engines.

At the speed the *Kronprinz Wilhelm* was making in her dash for life, the engines churned and thundered like so many living beasts, as in the rising sea the ship was restlessly tossing. From time to time I heard the racing of the propellers and the thud as they plunged back into the sea, and I thought in what a plight we would be if suddenly one should snap off. A thousand times had I been in such engine rooms, in smooth weather and in storm, but never before did the busy confusion of the moving powerful parts make me feel so gloomy.

"War is on," I kept saying to myself. "Even now we are being chased. How long will we have to rush madly about the sea, imprisoned in an inferno like this?" It was li..e an unpleasant dream.

When I came on deck I found that Commander Thierfelder was losing no time in beginning those preparations which soon put our ship into a neat state of offence and defence. Our mission as vessel of war was to capture and sink enemy merchant craft, first taking over whatever coal or provisions we needed, while being especially careful of the safety of passengers and crews. Our orders were to treat the passengers like guests, giving them first-class accommodations when possible, and showing them every courtesy discipline allowed. The captured crews should have second-class accommodations and were to be treated with the consideration accorded to prisoners of war. The fare of all on board should be the same, so that no captive would be able to complain that he had received meaner food than any of our seamen. In fact, it was our own seamen who later complained that the prisoners were getting better food than they, which made necessary an open reassurance on the part of the commander that no partiality was being shown.

But I am anticipating.

For the present Commander Thierfelder's efforts were centred chiefly on preparations for defence. His first care was to render bullet- and shrapnel-proof those vulnerable parts of the vessel exposed to hostile fire. For this purpose the men were filching from the hold all available mattresses, carpets, and bagging—robbing right and left without respect to rank or feelings—the consolation given was that we should soon capture a new supply from an enemy ship—and nailing them over the woodwork where they would do most good. The panels below the windows of the bridge were being thickly padded in this manner, the order being given that these glass windows should be taken out and stored away the instant "Clear for action!" sounded. The bulwarks and inner walls of the various decks were also being padded so as to protect sharpshooters stationed behind the bull's-eyes, while the smoking room, which was soon to be transformed into a hospital, was being given especial mattress protection. Should the woodwork in any vital part of the ship be struck by hostile bullets the splinters would be caught by these paddings before they could do harm.

A second alteration fully as important as these was also going forward. As our vessel when at high speed burned five hundred tons of coal daily, and as we could not depend upon a regular replenishment of supply, Commander Thierfelder considered it necessary to create more bunker space. The ship's carpenters were accordingly dismantling the now purposeless grand saloon, which from a chamber of palatial magnificence was thus brutally metamorphosed into a reserve coal bin.

I remember with what a pang I suddenly came upon the beginning of this work. Just as I appeared at the grand stairway, the great mirrors were being taken down, and the empty walls behind them looked as if they were gasping for breath. I felt like a man who watches the workmen begin to tear down his old home. Only a short time had I been on the *Kronprinz Wilhelm,* but in that space I had never tired of coming to this spacious hall so magnificently decorated and so luxuriously furnished. The grand stairways on either side had seemed to lead to the floor of some fabulous cavern of wealth; while the carpets, the tapestries, the marble-furnished walls, exhibited luxury beyond human use. It was here I could imagine a banquet of the ancient gods ranged round almighty Jove with graceful Hebe filling the golden goblets. Only the day before I had sat back in the plush cushions gazing round me with a feeling of unlimited possession, while only the faint and far-off rumble of the engines and the never-ceasing tremor of the ship as she rose and fell on the unstable sea reminded me that I was not in Eden or Empyrean but on the tempestuous war-darkened ocean.

"This is war," I grumbled when I saw all this splendour vanish. "War alone would permit this blasphemy—war, the destroyer."

From the grand saloon I went to the smoking room to find a similar course of work in progress. This room, which so many former passengers on the *Kronprinz Wilhelm* will remember as their cozy place of refuge from the chatter and gossip of their fairer fellow voyagers, was rapidly being remodelled into the ship's hospital. In place of mahogany bookcases, tables, and chairs rows of bunks, hospital benches, and medicine cabinets were being erected; while the walls, as before mentioned, were being padded with mattresses as a protection against flying splinters.

Shortly after sunset that night as, busied with the progress of alterations, the ship still rushed along in her eastward flight, the gong sounded suddenly, and the bugle blew to station. I ran up on deck and looking to starboard beheld on the horizon the lights of a ship. The crow's nest warned that a fast French cruiser was bearing down upon us. Commander Thierfelder, who expected no friends in this part of the sea, had already ordered the helm about, and the *Kronprinz Wilhelm* was turning to port.

Again it was a race for life, this time by night. The

hostile cruiser had come up due east of us; in a few minutes more we had turned directly toward the west and were putting on every ounce of steam.

In an open battle with the Frenchman the *Kronprinz Wilhelm* with her two tiny guns—as yet not in their emplacement—and mattress armour must have fallen a speedy prey. Commander Thierfelder also had vowed never to surrender the ship—an oath we felt he could be depended on to keep. So our only hope lay in a good pair of heels.

During the first few minutes of this chase the cruiser seemed to gain upon us. Already her searchlights had been maliciously placed, sweeping the sea about us, so that for a time as we sped along we thought we were within range, fearing at every instant that the first few shots would drop into our hold and blow us to the skies. But the *Kronprinz Wilhelm* proved the faster ship. By degrees we laid greater distance between us; soon the Frenchman was definitely out of range and perceptibly losing ground, and in an hour the hostile lights had sunk from sight.

The *Kronprinz Wilhelm*, however, was by no means safe. In the wireless room Lieutenant Brinkmann was intercepting messages from the Frenchman, which notified all other Allied warships of our position. There was no doubt that this part of the sea was well policed, so that at any minute we might expect lights on our quarter or our bow.

Luckily, the night was dark and the heavens overcast,

We, of course, were running without lights, while every chink in our sides which might let out a telltale ray was kept as carefully covered as on our first sailing from Hoboken. It was a law of the ship that anyone found negligent in the matter of lights at night would be tried for treason. But this warning was superfluous. The men took such personal interest in the safety of the vessel that they noted all points of danger, reporting them at once.

On this dark night of our chase into the unknown west no enemy could have seen us save at short range. For four hours we steamed at full speed without slackening; then Commander Thierfelder began a zigzag course at slower speed toward the south.

I was so tired when I finally got to my bunk that I told one of the orderlies, Mathias Schiffers, to wake me before sunup, and not to leave my bunk's side until he had gotten me up. This precaution was well taken. For I seemed but to have closed my eyes when someone tugged at my sleeve.

"Time to get up, Lieutenant." It was Schiffer's voice.

"What, already!"

"Yes, sir. It's three-thirty."

I got up grumbling. But the boy was right. The sky was already beginning to show signs of dawn.

I went out on deck and up on the bridge. Commander Thierfelder was still there, having been up all night with a few other officers. All were anxiously scanning the sea for traces of the enemy. If, when dawn broke, the French cruiser or other enemy warships should be in sight, we were lost. The mantle of night might save us, but in an all-day chase, with the enemy so numerous and in wireless communication, we would surely be rounded up before the end of day.

As light began to break, practically all the ship's officers were on the different bridges scanning the horizon. Each faint freak of the sky became for the moment an optical illusion; some thought they saw smoke in the distance, and I, too, had my misgivings about some clouds on the horizon. As day dawned brighter, however, it became clear that the *Kronprinz Wilhelm* was alone on the blue ocean. We breathed freely again. Our enemy had been lost in the night.

Lieutenant Fix, a man deliberate of speech and of few words, shook hands with the commander.

"Congratulations, Commander," he said.

"Yes," Commander Thierfelder answered, "that was a close shave."

That morning at about eleven o'clock the whole crew assembled on the aft deck to listen to a talk by the commander.

Commander Thierfelder was a clean-shaven young man, only thirty years old, of middle height, quiet and retiring in his ways, but quick and firm in his actions. He had already acquired a reputation among us for keeping to himself. When off duty he seemed never to be about ship, but if needed was usually found in his stateroom reading a classic. When on duty, on the other hand, he was singularly alert, his blue eyes moving quickly about taking in every detail, while his face in contrast remained placid, without sign of emotion. When he spoke, he looked directly into the eyes with a glance that was not to be evaded. Before an assembly he spoke slowly, quietly, and with good intonation but with few gestures, much as if reciting; yet the continuity and brevity of his speech were such that the attention could not stray.

On this occasion he spoke upon the mission of the *Kronprinz Wilhelm* as a commerce destroyer.

"Men of German blood," he said, "your Fatherland has chosen you for a high duty—that of harassing the commerce of the enemy—thus making it harder for him to continue war against your brothers in the trenches. Our duty is to sink merchant ships, at the same time taking due care of the safety of their passengers and crew.

"Remember, men, we hope soon to begin our captures; then the time of temptation and self-control will begin. On the ships we take will be valuables, intoxicants, and women." Here a laugh went up, but quickly subsided when it was apparent that the commander was not joking.

"The valuables are the common prize of the ship and must be given up to be raffled off later among the whole crew. The intoxicants shall be delivered up untouched upon pain of court-martial. Let not one drunken seaman disgrace the voyage of the *Kronprinz Wilhelm*. And last, men, the women. Remember your mothers, your wives, your sisters. I need say no more.

"During the last twenty-four hours we have twice had a hard chase and by the grace of God are for the present safe. I noted that in the emergency each man did his duty. Continue in future to show the same spirit, and at the end, whether here or in heaven, your reward will come."

After he had finished, all were silent. Then Lieutenant Hoffmann, in his lively fashion, stepped out.

"Men," he shouted, his hand raised high. *"Hoch!* to Commander Thierfelder."

Instantly, every man was on his feet cheering at the top of his voice. In answer Commander Thierfelder bowed, then stood quiet until the cheering had ceased, when he spoke slowly: "Save your cheers," he said, "until we take our first ship."

Chapter IV

WE RECEIVE COAL AND A STOWAWAY
FROM THE "WALHALLA"

HOW soon would we take our first ship and of what nationality would it be? These were now subjects both for speculation and betting. I had lost a box of cigars to Lieutenant Hoffmann since the *Kronprinz Wilhelm* had become a ship of war. He now bet me we would capture an enemy craft within a week, which bet I took as I had the first—for the sake of the argument.

It was now the ninth of August. We had been upon the seas six days, in which short space the *Kronprinz Wilhelm* had been put into fairly good shape for her mission. The ship had been totally repainted, her mattress armour perfected, the saloon coal bin constructed, the smoking-room hospital placed in readiness; and, most important of all, the two 88 mm. guns bolted to their emplacements.

These two guns fast became the pride of the ship. One of them, which the crew baptized the White Arrow, was stationed on the port side of the forecastle, sweeping an angle of 180 degrees. The other, which, because of its deep tone when discharged, the crew dubbed the Base Drum, was placed on the starboard side opposite its mate

—it also had a sweep of 180 degrees. Thus armed, the *Kronprinz Wilhelm* could bring one gun into play on whichever side an enemy appeared. In addition, our machine gun, which the crew called the Riveter because its discharge sounded like the metallic drumming of a riveting machine, was stationed on the middle bridge, where it could be carried to either side of the ship as the emergency might demand.

Daily the gun crews—all men who had seen previous service—were put through an exhilarating drill. Little ammunition, however, was used as our supply was too small. Instead, empty cartridges were used, the men thus getting the practice of action without diminishing our supply of ammunition. The crew worked enthusiastically, trained the guns as seriously as if an enemy were the target, and soon showed such proficiency that Hoffmann wanted to meet an enemy if only to prove that our men could shoot. He tried to bet me that the White Arrow would make the first hit; when I refused he offered to reverse the bet, championing the cause of the Base Drum.

That was Hoffmann to the core. Above all he was anxious to see action. It was my friend's one wish—expressed to me in private and without boasting—to be placed in such a position that he could die for his country. I never saw a more patriotic youth. His one thought was always: "This will help or this will injure my Fatherland." To the heart he was a German and, as I know, prayed sincerely that when he died it might be in behalf of his country.

Hoffmann, you had your wish. Whether right or wrong is not for me to say: you are gone, and God knows you went not in pursuit of your own interests.

Lieutenant Brinkmann, our wireless expert, had by this time caught messages from London which stated that Montenegro had also entered the war. The conflagration had spread over all Europe and it seemed might go still farther. We began to feel that in such an involved affair perhaps the issue would not come so fast. However confident of victory my fellow officers might feel, and, even though I had seen enough of European military life to regard the German armies as invincible, I nevertheless felt that the country's isolation might in the long run starve her into submission. These thoughts, however, I kept to myself as they were tantamount to treason.

At any rate, I had a subconscious feeling that the struggle would not be short, so that I began to look upon our two guns, our mattress armour, our camouflage, and our saloon coal bin as more or less permanent features which would either be carried about with us for ever so long or go to the bottom in the end. In fact, the *Kronprinz Wilhelm* had completely laid aside the appearance of a peaceful passenger vessel and had taken on the aspect of a converted man-of-war.

The ship itself did not give this impression so much as the naval drill and the bearing of officers and crew. The former gave their orders no longer in that quiet, half-indulgent manner peculiar to officers on passenger liners, but in sharp, curt commands; the latter, on the other hand, dropped all familiarity, stood back as men must in the navy, obeying on the instant, under the articles of war.

On the same ninth of August Commander Thierfelder caused all members of the crew who had not formerly been in the German naval or military service to take the oath of allegiance. Those whose duties were not already prescribed were now divided into three general groups. Of the first a ship's guard of gunners and sharpshooters was formed. These manned the two guns and machine gun or were given stations behind bulwarks and bull's-eyes, with rifles for close-range attack. The second group constituted a munition train, whose duties were to supply the ship's guard with ammunition in time of action. The third group consisted of the stretcher and hospital corps. This completed our warlike character. The *Kronprinz Wilhelm* was now ready for a fight.

A victim, however, did not show itself speedily. From the ninth to the seventeenth of August we continued our southeasterly course without sighting a sail. The men were kept busy perfecting preparations, still making minor alterations in our hold and wielding the paint brush whenever an opportune moment allowed. Daily the different corps went through their drills and everything began running as smoothly as a machine.

On the night of the seventeenth we reached the Azores and rounded San Miguel. Here, as our wireless warned us, lay numerous enemy battleships. We knew almost their exact locations, and fearing that their submarine instruments might detect our presence by the pulsations of our propellers we put on all speed to run by them in the dark.

Had we been at liberty to choose our direction, Commander Thierfelder would never have run into these dangerous waters. The *Kronprinz Wilhelm,* however, had made arrangements by wireless to meet the German ship *Walhalla* in latitude 35 degrees north, longitude 25 degrees west, which was just below the Azores, and the only route the commander could choose to reach the friendly ship at the time agreed upon lay directly through the jaws of the enemy. But under cover of night, if all went well, the chances of slipping through were good.

In the wireless room Lieutenant Brinkmann and his corps of assistants were all on the watch. By means of delicate instruments the young lieutenant was able to tell the approximate distance and direction of any ship sending out wireless messages. He kept a map constantly before him, charted out the probable positions of enemy ships, interpolated when he thought his readings in error, and by this means gave Commander Thierfelder as clear a map of enemy danger spots as if he were looking down upon the sea from the moon through a telescope. And I must give Brinkmann this credit—that not once in the course of our voyage did we find his charts in error. At a later period, when the seas were being combed for us by eighty Allied warships scattered over the Atlantic, he steered us out of danger by means of his instruments and his shrewd deductions. When we finally did almost run into a warship, as I shall later recount, it was because the enemy, like us, had refrained from using her wireless, being thus beyond Brinkmann's detections.

Fortunately for the *Kronprinz Wilhelm,* she thus had in Lieutenant Brinkmann a man whose genius seemed to lend itself to anything connected with wireless. With ease and precision he could tell the names of ships talking with each other, for he had a remarkable talent for identifying the intensity, rapidity, "tone," and "colour" of the pulsations of their respective wireless waves.

"That's the *Bristol,*" he would say. "That's the *Eiffel;* that's the *Sayville;* that's the *Leipzig*"; and so on—always cocksure.

Then, he had a genius for deciphering an unknown code when supplied with a dozen or so messages in it. His method, as far as he could explain it, was not unlike that of Edgar Allan Poe, the American poet, as given in his story "The Gold Bug," but when we had asked the last of our questions we were forced to conclude that Brinkmann was as much a wireless genius as some men are chess or mathematical prodigies. He knew simply by instinct.

It was naturally a distinct advantage to the *Kronprinz Wilhelm* to have as its wireless officer a man like Brinkmann at a time when we were being sought by the enemy on every portion of the Atlantic. Later I shall show how Brinkmann's resourcefulness made us able to outwit enemy ships to our advantage.

When he met us at mess, Brinkmann, one of my nearest friends, was in the habit of telling Hoffmann and me any important messages received during the previous watch. This night as we steamed past the Azores he had been particularly busy. The enemy was talking business the whole time. Unfortunately, I did not make notes of all Brinkmann told us, but I remember that the British Admiralty had telegraphed that it had reason to believe a squadron of German cruisers under command of Admiral Count von Spee to be in these waters.

This was hailed as good news. Our hopes rose that we might fall in with the German squadron. Brinkmann, however, doubted the fact, while Commander Thierfelder indicated that we must be especially cautious about mistaking enemy ships for our own. In fact, he believed that some Allied cruisers would disguise themselves as German warships the better to decoy into capture just such commerce destroyers as ourselves. He cautioned Brinkmann against answering a message coming to us in the secret German code, as the code might have gotten into the enemy's possession. For this reason Brinkmann refused to answer a number of messages from the *Karlsruhe* and other German vessels which reached us from the southern seas, although he felt certain of the identity of the ships.

Our dash past the Azores at last neared its end. Thus far, although we had run within thirty miles of Allied warships, we had not come in sight of one. Our commander, ever on the alert and in constant telephonic touch with

Brinkmann, steered us rapidly to the south. In the next few hours we would again be out of danger.

I must not forget to mention that during this night and the two preceding we beheld the eastern sky lit up intermittently in a sparkling fashion, as if with electric discharges. The officers were of the opinion that the illumination was heat lightning such as is often seen in these latitudes after a sultry day, but the men persisted in the belief that the light resulted from a reflection in the heavens of the cannon flashes of their comrades and enemies on land hundreds of miles away—a mirage. Considering the distance, this was preposterous, but the belief took fast hold. It was impossible to reason with the men, who wanted to explain the phenomenon in that way, and who thought they had plausible evidence upon which to base their belief. We soon gave up trying; and to this day when I meet one of our survivors, he usually reminds me of these lights, stubbornly arguing with me if I attempt to disagree.

The night of the Azores was fast waning when most of the officers turned in for a nap. I stayed on to watch until morning. It had been a nerve-straining night even to men by this time accustomed to the excitement of watching in dangerous waters. In the morning, if all went well, we hoped to meet the *Walhalla*.

Our need of this ship was great. Already we were dangerously short of coal, and, though our provisions still held, an additional supply would give us greater security. Our water supply was also low, though not, as at later times, to the point of danger. But, above all, we were hungry for news. We had been on the sea almost two weeks, and, though our wireless gave us brief scraps of fact, yet we had only the most meagre knowledge of the happenings of the Great War on land and sea. No one can imagine how tantalizing brief bulletins caught from enemy cruisers can be in a crisis such as this. By the time we rounded the Azores there was not an officer aboard who would not have pawned his last possession for some news from home. It was for this reason that we looked forward to meeting the *Walhalla* with so much suspense.

Tuesday morning, the eighteenth of August, again found all officers on deck before dawn, waked from their naps to keep a lookout for enemy craft. To imagine what were our thoughts as we watched, it must be borne in mind that if but a single enemy cruiser should be in sight at dawn we would be caught and sunk before night. Our anxieties that morning, however, were soon relieved. Day broke and within the horizon was nothing but an endless waste of sea. We were safely past the dangerous Azores.

Now, however, another anxiety arose. For some time we had been wondering whether the *Walhalla* herself would safely reach the rendezvous. If she were discovered by the enemy while on her way to us, we might search for her in vain; if the enemy discovered her at the rendezvous, he would suspect her purpose and lay a trap for the vessel which should come to meet her; if the *Walhalla* had been captured, she might be left in the stipulated position as a decoy. It was of such a trap as this which Commander Thierfelder had to beware.

So we steamed along cautiously at a ten-mile speed, ready to dash away on the slightest suspicion. Our lookouts as usual manned the two stations of the foremast, training their glasses in every direction. At nine twenty o'clock the crow's nest discerned a faint haze of smoke over the *Walhalla* rendezvous, and ten minutes later the call came down that the single funnel of the *Walhalla* had appeared on the horizon.

Commander Thierfelder now reduced our speed to five miles; then, leaving the bridge, climbed into the lookout. Training his glasses on the *Walhalla,* he kept them riveted on the ship. In a short time he lowered them and came back on the bridge, and for the first time in days I saw him smile.

"All safe," he commented briefly. "Her signals are up."

The *Walhalla,* in short, had sighted us, and, not wishing to use her wireless, was displaying signal flags. Both our vessels now put on greater speed so that in half an hour the *Walhalla* had reached us.

There were great cheers from our boys as the vessel came alongside our port and made fast, and great disappointment when each crew learned that the other had no news to tell. For the *Walhalla* had put to sea before we left Hoboken, and her crew had been looking forward to hearing news from us with hopes equal to our own. We soon forgot our disappointments, however, in the pleasure of meeting old friends. Hands were shaken, experiences briefly told, and tradings made.

The captain of the *Walhalla* reported that he had lain in this same spot for the last fourteen days without sighting a ship, so that we might consider ourselves in a safe pocket of the ocean. Commander Thierfelder consequently felt justified in beginning to coal without running farther south. Our ships were kept together by a hawser across the lips of our bows, supplemented by a few lines across our poop, and a speed of two miles was maintained by both ships. This kept our noses together, gave us a certain steadiness in the unquiet water, and above all kept us constantly prepared, steamed up, to dash away in case an enemy cruiser appeared. It should also be mentioned that at each of the cables which held our ships together a man was stationed, ax in hand, to cut the hempen cable should the emergency arise.

Our preparations for coaling on the high seas had of course already been made. Through the decks of the *Kronprinz Wilhelm* we had cut large circular holes, one directly under the other, and, inserting the ship's ventilator tubes, had spliced them together in such a manner that when the coal was dumped on deck it merely had to be pushed into the tubes to slide swiftly down into the bunkers. Three temporary derricks had been erected, one fore, another midships, the third aft, all electrically equipped, later to be supplemented by electric winches taken from captured vessels. By using sacks and baskets loaded on the *Walhalla* and transferred from her derricks to our derricks in mid-air, we took aboard in the next three days twenty-five hundred tons of coal—enough to keep us going a week at good speed or two weeks at low speed. Before this coal should be used, we hoped to capture another supply from some Allied merchantman.

As we thus dropped down farther toward the tropics, the weather became increasingly warmer. So hot was the work of coaling that the men worked only in pantaloons, cut short like boys' trousers, or even in tights. There were of course no feminine eyes around, if we except the ship's cats, so that often even the scant loin cloths were cast aside, and the men worked naked. Covered from head to foot with sweaty coal dust, they soon looked like inhabitants of Africa. We officers fared as badly, for, though we were spared manual labour and so did not take off our clothes, do what we would our white uniforms became black in the course of a morning.

On the first day of our coaling I saw a young slip of a youth, one of the *Walhalla's* cabin boys, come aboard our ship. He was off duty, apparently making a friendly visit. He seemed slightly nervous, however, though I did not think anything of this at the moment. After speaking with some of our crew and being shown over the ship, he at last came up to me, saluted, and asked if he might not speak with the commander. Astonished at the request, I asked particulars. He said he wanted to be transferred to our ship as he was ambitious to share our glory.

"In that case," I answered, "I think you can see the commander. But I'd advise you to think twice before deciding. We're all doomed men on this ship—a kind of forlorn hope out here on the Atlantic."

The boy introduced himself to the commander as Karl Sturm of Hamburg. At his first words, however, Commander Thierfelder shook his head.

"Impossible," he said. "You're too young."

"I'm fifteen, sir."

"Fifteen is too young. Impossible."

Then the boy, reading in Commander Thierfelder's glance a good heart, made an eloquent plea for himself, telling how much he wanted to do something for his country, and ending by affirming that he was as good a man as any aboard ship. But Commander Thierfelder remained firm. The boy was too young for our service, and although he displayed exceptional spirit we could not take him aboard.

"Sorry, little brother," I said as we came down from the bridge.

He looked straight ahead, said nothing, and, saluting, quickly left the ship. As I ordered him to go over the side, I could not help thinking: "I'd like to see that chap aboard the *Kronprinz Wilhelm*. He looks as if he had grit."

When I told Hoffmann about the lad, that spirited fellow dismissed the subject in his characteristic way:

"I'd like to bet he'll sneak aboard as a stowaway."

I shrugged my shoulders, and we soon forgot about the ambitious Karl Sturm.

Coaling from the *Walhalla* was completed at noon of the twenty-first. In addition to fuel we had also taken aboard a goodly supply of provisions and fresh water. Our crew began to feel much as does a man who has a full coal bin in the fall. He need not worry. He is supplied. Only, there was the ever-hovering anxiety that at any moment destruction might come.

The *Walhalla* was at last ready to leave. On the previous day Commander Thierfelder had notified our crew that all men too old to be liable to military service would shortly be ordered aboard the *Walhalla,* which would take them back to land. I think there were many on board who envied these lucky men, yet there were also some among those about to leave us who went under protest.

As the hour of parting drew near, our men gathered around their departing companions, gave them letters to take home, shook hands, embraced, said good-bye many times, and helped them over the side. There was a genial mingling of sentiment and good cheer.

After the last man was over and the *Walhalla* was getting ready to let go, a female fox terrier came galloping over the vessel's deck, whining and yelping up to our men who were ranged along our rail. The dog had been brought aboard us each day of our coaling, had been much fed and petted by our crew, and now, evidently knowing that she was leaving us, was affectionately protesting. One of the officers of the *Walhalla,* seeing this, stepped up to his captain and spoke a few words. In an instant he was back

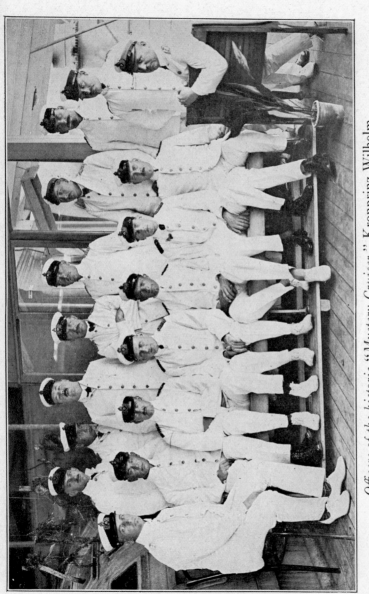

Officers of the historic "Mystery Cruiser," Kronprinz Wilhelm

again, he stooped, picked the dog up by the collar and tossed her to our deck.

"A present to the *Kronprinz Wilhelm* from the captain and crew of the *Walhalla!*" he shouted.

At once a great shout went up, followed by hearty cheers from our crew, while the bewildered dog pranced about our feet fawning and ingratiating herself until she was taken up into the arms of one of our men. Accordingly, in the name of the *Walhalla,* we adopted Nelka as one of our mascots. Nelka later on showed her gratitude by presenting us with charming little puppies.

As the *Walhalla* left our side, her crew and ours lined the rail or climbed up on the smokestacks and masts to wave hats and cheer across to each other, while our band struck up a patriotic air. The *Walhalla* put on all steam to the west and was soon but a speck upon the horizon, while we put on steam toward the south, so that in less than half an hour the friendly ship had disappeared. We learned later that she safely put into Las Palmas, where many of our crew aboard her again shipped, under feigned names, in the hope of reaching home.

The *Walhalla* had hardly disappeared when, as I was returning from the bridge to go below decks, I almost ran into a slim little form on his way up on deck. It was Karl Sturm, the boy who had so earnestly besought Commander Thierfelder to let him stay aboard as a member of our crew.

"Here, you!" I began. "Where do you come from?"

"Sir," he stammered, turning his hat in his hand, "I am aboard the *Kronprinz Wilhelm,* am I not?"

"I should say so. And the *Walhalla* is over there." I waved my hand toward the horizon.

The boy began to grin.

"I see," I said. "You went below decks on the *Kronprinz Wilhelm,* thought you'd take a rest in one of our cabins, and so fell asleep."

The boy continued to grin.

"Maybe the *Kronprinz Wilhelm* will overtake the *Walhalla* and put me aboard again," he said brazenly.

"Maybe," I answered. "Meanwhile, perhaps we'd better go up to Commander Thierfelder and ask him."

The boy continued to grin.

"Sir," he began, suddenly becoming serious, as he followed me, "if you'd please be so kind, it might help if the commander knew that I'm a good sailor."

"He will know you have one qualification at least," I retorted. "You've a good lot of nerve."

In another minute we were on the bridge. Commander Thierfelder gave one look at the approaching stowaway and without asking a further question turned quietly to me.

"Count," he said, "take him below and tell the bosun to give him a berth and find out what he's fit for."

"You got off easily," I suggested as I accompanied the boy below decks.

"He looks like a good one," retorted the boy.

"He'll treat you square. Now, what are you good for?"

"Anything." The boy looked up proudly.

"How would you like the signal corps?"

"Sir, I should like that more than anything else."

"Well, you look bright. Keep your liking to yourself and I'll try to get you into that service."

I soon arranged the matter and Karl Sturm, our only stowaway, became a member of our signal corps, in which branch he rose rapidly, finally so distinguishing himself that the German Admiralty awarded him an Iron Cross second class.

When I got back to Commander Thierfelder, he confirmed my disposal of the boy.

"He looks like the right sort of chap," I remarked.

"Yes," Commander Thierfelder answered. "I'm glad he came aboard."

This concluded the incidents of the *Walhalla* rendezvous. The *Kronprinz Wilhelm* now put her nose to the wind to search in earnest for hostile prey.

Chapter V

WE SPARE THE RUSSIAN "PITTAN" AND HUNT RATS

A N EARNEST search for enemy ships it certainly
was. Already we had been at sea the best part of a
month, and though our achievements in eluding capture
and converting the ship upon the high seas were not incon-
siderable, yet this was not the mission upon which the
Kronprinz Wilhelm had left the safe harbour of Hoboken.
Her business was to sink enemy ships, and thus far we had
not captured a single ton.

But it should not be out of place here to remind the
American reader that the events which took place on the
Kronprinz Wilhelm fell within the very first quarter of
the great World War and were ended almost two years
before America had even thought of entering the contest.
At no time did the *Kronprinz Wilhelm* come into conflict
with an American right, at no time did she raise an issue
between the German and American governments—at no
time, in short, did there exist any other than the most
cordial feelings between our crew and the American people.
And, as the sequel will show, it was to America alone

that we at last felt free to turn to entrust our imperilled safety.

The *Walhalla,* as I said before, had not sighted a single ship during her two weeks' wait in this rendezvous. Commander Thierfelder, therefore, not expecting to make any captures in this locality, bore off to the southwest to run along a South American sea lane. We had not gone far in this direction when on the twenty-seventh of August at 2 P. M., to the agreeable surprise of officers and men, our lookout sighted a schooner to port. Five minutes later a second schooner appeared on the horizon some leagues farther south. These would be our first prizes.

We singled out the nearest vessel for attack, put on a leisurely speed so as not to waste coal, and in an hour had come within hail. Our prize was a little three-masted schooner under full sail, bearing gallantly onward before a ten-mile breeze. As we came near, we beheld at her masthead the Danish colours. Accordingly, if she bore no contraband, our first ship would be no prize at all. We would have to let her proceed.

When we had come within a few hundred yards, Commander Thierfelder signalled to the vessel to stop and questioned her, receiving the captain's assurance that his ship was the Danish schooner *Elizabetha* of Fanoe, and was carrying a noncontraband cargo. As everything seemed to bear out the truth of these statements and we had no time to lose, I thought the commander would let the schooner go and proceed to the taking of the second sailing vessel.

Commander Thierfelder, however, was nothing if not thorough. For all the schooner's innocent looks and the apparent honesty of her captain she might, nevertheless, contain contraband. Furthermore, her crew might give us news of other vessels which would aid us in a capture or in avoiding danger. A prize boat was accordingly sent over to her.

One of our officers was soon aboard the *Elizabetha* examining the ship's papers and inspecting her cargo. All proved to be as the captain had reported. He added that he had not sighted a sail in a fortnight, save the schooner now in view. Commander Thierfelder, satisfied with the report, signalled to the *Elizabetha* to proceed and then steamed off in pursuit of the second sail. This time he hoped to be in better luck.

The ship we were nearing, a homely three-master, had a neat white hull, in strange contrast with her patched and discoloured sails, and when we had come near enough we could see that she bore the marks of economy from stem to stern. At her masthead she either innocently or brazenly flew the Russian flag.

As I was watching her from the bridge, I noted one of our sailors climb upon our forecastle head, camera in hand.

"Ah," I thought, "I have been cursing my luck ever since we left Hoboken for forgetting to bring along films for my camera. Here is a man who has some."

I went over to the seaman. To my astonishment he told me with a laugh that a short time ago he had bought all the films aboard ship in order to possess the only pictures of the voyage.

"Nothing like monopoly," he grinned.

"What'll you take for them?" I asked.

At first he seemed reluctant to set a price, saying that he wanted to keep his monopoly, at least until some cameras should be captured, when his monopoly would no doubt come to an end. I surmised, however, that he would sell a part of them.

Just as I was on the point of closing for half of his films, a thought struck me: If a monopoly on the pictures of this voyage was so valuable to this man, why wouldn't it be equally valuable to me?

I accordingly changed my offer, saying I would buy all or none. Again he seemed unwilling but in the end set a high price. I bought his whole outfit including some pictures he had already taken the first part of the voyage.

While these negotiations were going on, the little schooner *Pittan* had stopped at our command. As we knew her to be Russian and accordingly an enemy, a prize crew was immediately sent over to her. There was no doubt we had found our first victim.

In charge of the prize crew was my friend Lieutenant Fix, who afterward told me all that happened on board the schooner.

As the prize boat neared the sailing vessel, the latter's captain came to the rail. He was a huge, unshaven Russian, the picture of what in America has become the cartoon for a Bolshevist. When our boat came near enough, Lieutenant Fix saw in the man's face a mixture of inquisitiveness and surprise. His crew, which had likewise come to the rail, eyed the oncoming boat with manifest wonder. They evidently could not understand why our large ship had condescended to order them to stop and was now sending a boat over to them. Perhaps we wanted to buy provisions, in which case their captain was most probably slyly gauging the kind of bargain he should drive.

Fix clambered up the side first, followed by his second officer, and in another instant was confronting the huge man.

"You are a prisoner of war," Fix began in the Russian tongue. "Give us your papers. We are going to sink your ship!"

"Sink my ship!" The man looked from one officer to the other in stupefaction. He could not believe the words. Behind him his crew showed by gestures of astonishment that they did not know war had been declared.

"Yes," continued Fix, "war is on between Russia and Germany. Your ship is an enemy. We are going to bring off your crew as prisoners of war, take whatever we need of your cargo, and then sink your ship."

As the Russian captain began to comprehend these words, his lips parted and he uttered a cry of despair. Falling on his knees, his hands raised imploringly to Fix, he begged, weeping to be let off. Fix told me he would never forget the tragedy written on the man's face.

"This ship is all I have," he sobbed. "I have worked years—saved, starved myself—to buy this ship. Now I'm ruined. My wife, my children—they will be penniless. I'm a ruined man. I'm a ruined man."

Fix is a soft-hearted fellow. He felt a pang of remorse to see this rugged giant on his knees humbly begging. He stooped and shook the man by the shoulder, trying to calm him, but the Russian continued to implore and sob until Fix told him he would go back to Commander Thierfelder and try to beg him off. Fix assured him there was good reason to believe he could manage this, since the *Pittan* was of little importance after all.

At these words the man rose, seized Fix's hands, tried to kiss them—a gesture which Fix courteously avoided—and, after giving up his papers, followed Fix to the ship's side, thanking him, yet still imploring, repeating again and again that the ship was all in the world he owned.

When these facts were brought before Commander Thierfelder, his face showed no change, but I, who had begun to understand him, knew that his sense of justice had been touched.

"He hasn't anything of much value on board," the commander said at last. "All right," he continued, handing the papers back to Fix. "Tell him he can go upon condition he will describe what ships he has seen in the last few weeks and promise not to write in his log of having met us. Tell him if we see him again we shall demand his log."

With this Fix again went over the side. The big Russian had been in such agony of suspense that he had put out in a lifeboat to meet our prize crew. When he heard what Fix reported he again shed tears—this time of joy. He at once told Fix of sighting a few ships—all, however, of little importance—and gladly promised he would not mention us in his log. And if we ever put into Riga, Fix should look him up. He would treat him handsomely.

As Fix was about to order his boat back to our side, the Russian suddenly called to him to wait. He had forgotten something. Stooping, he lifted out of his boat two one-gallon jugs, both evidently full of liquor.

"One for the gallant lieutenant," the Russian said effusively, "the other for the gallant captain."

Fix did not know whether to take the reward or not but, seeing that his refusal would only offend the man, took the offering of gratitude, thanked the captain, shook hands with him, answered his salute, and started back to our side. When he got out of hearing, he stopped his oarsmen to tell them that since an officer may not accept a present from an enemy the two jugs with what was in them were their own property, to be divided when they got aboard. Needless to say, the contents proved to be a fiery species of brandy, heartily enjoyed by the prize crew and their friends.

As we began to steam away from the spot, we noticed that the captain of the *Pittan* had manned the yards in our honour and that his crew was waving us good-bye. I tried to get a picture of the salute, but the smoke from our newly primed fires was constantly blown into my line of sight until we were too far away. The last thing of interest that I remember in connection with the vessel was seeing her rather large Russian flag suddenly begin to descend from the masthead by successive jerks, until it disappeared on deck. What flag the *Pittan* flew for the rest of her voyage, we never learned.

Our second ship had thus proved a disappointment. Nevertheless, a start had been made. The men had now twice gone through the process of sighting, approaching, and stopping a vessel; even though these ships were but schooners. The work of the *Kronprinz Wilhelm* seemed begun.

Foiled for the present, our energies were now turned in a different direction. One of our officers on his regular tour of inspection had noted a few days before that the rats, of which there are numbers aboard all vessels, had made ravages into the woodwork of our life rafts and the cork belts of our boats despite every effort to destroy them. Now, the boat's deck of the *Kronprinz Wilhelm,* in addition to carrying some twenty rafts, held as many large lifeboats for use in an emergency. The rafts were wooden platforms bolted to hollow cylinders—in many cases of wood covered with canvas. Into these cylinders the rats gnawed their way to make nests and places of refuge. The lifeboats, on the other hand, were fitted with six-inch life belts which ran lengthwise along the gunwale. Into these life belts the rats had burrowed, throwing on deck the sawdustlike bits of cork.

Commander Thierfelder accordingly decided that now in the interval of waiting for a prize was a good time to exterminate these pests. A war party was organized, consisting of about a hundred sailors—practically a whole division—and I was placed in command of the hunt.

I ordered all men to equip themselves with sticks, stiff rope ends, or any other weapon adapted to the hunt, and in addition to bring to the boat's deck some loose oakum. When the men arrived, they presented a singular appearance. Some carried sticks stolen from the fireroom; others bore canes; a few had ropes; but the majority had taxed their ingenuity inventing distinctive contrivances peculiar to their respective genius. One had the leg of a pair of pantaloons tightly twisted and wound with cord, a lump of coal tied into one end making the weapon resemble an enormous blackjack. Another carried a crabbing net in one hand and the leg of a stool in the other. A third brought a monkey wrench, the head of which was wound with oakum and tied with rope to keep the steel from injuring the deck. Still another had borrowed a tennis racket which some seaman with a sense of the incongruous had brought on board; this the men had wound with rope, so converting it into a solid paddle. Most individual of all, one fellow carried a frying pan, borrowed from the galley, with which in the end he executed as many rats as anyone else.

Then added to the distinctiveness of the weapons was the easy deshabille of the men's attire. For, as the sun's heat had become almost tropical, each man wore only his hat and his coaling trousers—the latter cut off at the knees. In all, the ratters looked most formidable.

Our hunting dogs were two fiery-eyed ferrets which the ship carried both as pets and for ratting. These trained and valuable animals were the property of Captain Grahn, who had bought them in New York of a man who offered to rid the ship of rats in return for a first-class passage to Europe—an offer which the sudden outbreak of war had cancelled. Two of our men held these quick little ferrets tucked in their hats.

I now ordered all hands to fall to with the loose oakum and stop up every hole into which or out of which a rat might scurry. This caulking the men did quickly, discovering holes in rafts which at a casual glance seemed flawless. All work of preparation ended, I took the men aft where I made a cordon of them across the ship behind the last funnel. We would start at the stern and work forward, cleaning one section at a time.

Just as we were about to begin, a bright idea came to one of the men.

"Let's have the cats up, Lieutenant," he suggested, "and watch the fun."

This suggestion was immediately seconded by the rest; so, despite my misgivings, I ordered a half-dozen men off to bring up our seven cats. Meantime, someone else, inspired by a sense of mischief, suggested bringing up Nelka, our newly acquired mascot of the *Walhalla*. This proposition was also seconded in chorus, and not wanting to discourage the men by a refusal I dispatched two men to get the dog.

While the cat and dog parties were thus on their way, the crew called for a song leader, and one Schmitt stepped forth. Schmitt, a master at improvisation, proved his adaptability on this occasion by chanting a chorus to a drinking song. The crew drank it in greedily and boisterously repeated it. It ended, so far as I can remember, something like this :

"Rat, tat, tat,
We'll smite him with our hat;
And if he will not slumber then,
We'll hit him on the head again,
Rat, tat, tat,
We'll smite him with our hat."

The men with the animals had now begun to arrive. They brought cats of all colours. The cats, not knowing what the excitement was about, became frightened and tried to get away; but after being turned at liberty in the centre of a ring of men they soon fell to looking about, scratching fleas, and sniffing along the deck.

In the midst of this Nelka was brought up. The dog had become much excited by being hurried along in the arms of her escorts, so that when she was suddenly dropped into the circle with the seven cats the animal almost lost her wits.

On the instant the cats scattered; then turned about at sight of only one enemy to set up an impressive yowling and hissing; after which, having roused their courage as well as their fur, they of one accord menacingly began to close in upon the helpless enemy. The unlucky and really peaceful-minded dog made a few quick turns to escape, encountered a cat at each turn, looked helplessly up into the eyes of the men as if to say: "Why do you torment me thus?"—then turned with a yelp upon the nearest cat to give battle.

This completely baffled that particular cat, which escaped hissing between the legs of the sailors, while at the same time one of the men—all of them were enjoying the sport as something not on the programme—stooped and picked the dog up in his arms.

This ended the episode.

The first red-eyed ferret was now put down before one of the holes in the cylinder of a raft, while a sailor pulled out the oakum caulking. When the man took his hand away, the little beast sniffed a minute, cautiously thrust its head into the hole, then quietly slipped into the cylinder. In an instant a confused squeaking became audible, and this at once brought some of the cats back upon the scene. Then out upon deck leaped a string of rats—one after the other so fast it seemed magic.

This was the beginning of general pandemonium. The cats pounced upon the first victims; the men with great ado began to flourish their frying-pan-tennis-racket-pants-leg weapons upon the scurrying pests, narrowly missing the cats and sometimes giving each other a stray blow. One of these afterward led to a fight below decks because the smitten sailor declared the blow intentional.

The uproar, however, was short-lived, and a minute later quiet reigned. The victims—eight in all—lay dead about the deck or were dangling by the tails from the fingers of sailors. No more rats came from the hole at which the cats now stood guard, their eyes fixed upon it while the tips of their tails lashed back and forth. Inside the cylinder all was as quiet as before we began. The work on that particular hole was evidently complete.

A sailor now punched oakum into the empty hole to prevent any of the pests from slipping in before the carpenters could repair the damage. As the second cylinder of this raft had no hole, we now went to the next, where the procedure was the same; this raft yielded five or six rats.

At the end of an exciting hour and a half we had cleaned the whole boat deck. Some twenty rats and mice had been killed and thrown overboard, while only a few had escaped to the deck below. Our casualties were one man bitten in the finger by a rat and another in the palm of the hand by one of the ferrets. These men received first-aid treatment from the hospital corps and were jocularly proclaimed the first aboard ship to win honour by being wounded in action. A few minor scratches from the excited cats, received at the time of the appearance of the dog, together with the stray blows of the awkward or mischievous ratters, were not counted. The cats and the ferrets seemed to have escaped unscathed.

By nightfall the number of rats caught had risen to a few hundred, the size of some of them—of course the ones which the narrator had himself slain—had expanded to the proportions of cats—indeed some of them were quite large—and the number dispatched by certain members of the crew had increased imposingly. Everyone is acquainted with this kind of psychology.

That evening at dusk our attention was momentarily drawn away from the rat hunt by the sighting of a sailing vessel. Through our glasses, however, we soon made out the American colours, and as we cherished only the best of feelings for Americans and wished above all to create no ill will, we did not even steam near to stop the craft.

Not until the night of the first of September did we sight another ship. On that night we almost ran into a hostile cruiser. The enemy was steaming with starboard lights to us, apparently not expecting a prize in these waters. As the night was not bright and we as usual were running in complete darkness, we were comparatively certain not to be seen.

Commander Thierfelder, however, took no chances. Pointing the *Kronprinz Wilhelm* directly toward the enemy

so as to show as little of the ship's hull as possible, he
stopped the engines. If, as was probable, the enemy should
be equipped with submarine signalling instruments, she
would now not be able to hear our propellers. Then, after
we had lain quiet for half an hour and the cruiser had disappeared, we again picked up our speed and steered away
over the cloudy sea.

It was Hoffmann's watch the first half of this night.

"Heinz," I said as I left him, "don't run us into the
British High Seas Fleet to-night." And as I went to my
cabin I thought how strange it would feel to be waked
from sleep by a tremendous explosion or by the waters of
the ocean rising over my head.

Chapter VI

THE "INDIAN PRINCE," THE FIRST
PRIZE OF THE WAR

I WAS awakened, however, by neither explosion nor water, but by the duteous voice of Mathias Schiffers calling me to get up. The *Kronprinz Wilhelm* that morning was rapidly nearing the equator.

Now it so happened that there were between sixty and seventy men aboard who had never crossed the line, and sailors' custom demands that every man crossing the equator for the first time must be baptized to the sea. This ceremony, one of the most jolly known to sea life, is called *Linientaufe,* or Line Baptism.

But I shall here crave your indulgence to reserve the story of this Line Baptism for a later chapter, when I shall give it at full length. Suffice it, we had a roaring time that day and late into the night.

Thursday morning, the third of September, broke upon a sunny sea. Yet despite the revelry of the evening before, all members of the proper watch were up and going about their routine as usual. After a few minutes' brisk walk on deck, to rouse an appetite, and a hearty breakfast, I went back to my room to write some notes in my diary concerning our *Linientaufe*.

While thus engaged, I happened to see lying in my cabinet a copy of the *Linientaufe Zeitung—Line Baptism Newspaper*—which had been printed on board the *Kronprinz Wilhelm* and distributed the day before, but which in the excitement of the hour I had only skimmed through. I dropped my pen and began reading.

The newspaper was a four-page affair. The front page, a kind of title page, bore the name of our ship and the date of the edition. Opening the leaves, I found the inner left-hand page filled with the drollest puns and jokes. On the page opposite came the news of the day, received by wireless. Of course, this news, like the premature notices of Mark Twain's death, was grossly exaggerated. One read here of all kinds of mysterious happenings. The Polish navy, if I remember rightly, had bombarded the fortified port of Berne, and a Chinese zeppelin had mounted so high while crossing the Alps on its trial trip from Peking that it collided with the Eiffel Tower and knocked off the flag pole which was caught by a quick Frenchman before it struck the ground, thus saving the honour of the Republic. Also a French general was announced as having surrendered a whole army corps out of revenge upon a lieutenant, his rival in love, on whom he intended to blame the catastrophe.

Then came a description of how the Russians trained their men to surrender. Each recruit was forced to exercise daily for three hours in the following manner: At the command "Company, surrender!" he threw down his gun and raised both hands vertically over his head, shouting at the top of his voice: "Kamerad! Kamerad!" If a man in this exercise lowered his hands or ceased shouting "Kamerad!" only an instant before the command to "Cease surrender!" was given he was forthwith taken before his company and shot on the spot as an example to the rest.

This nonsense, written approximately as my memory has given it, was so ably told that a dull wit might easily have accepted it as truth. Fortunately, our crew from humblest to highest was intelligent to say the least. I do not remember a single stupid man, unless it was the sailor who one calm day let one of my shoes fall overboard while polishing the pair for a consideration and then tried to explain the accident by saying that the ship had given a sudden lurch.

Equally well written were the announcements printed on the last page of the *Line Baptism Newspaper*. These ranged from advertisements asking for female cooks and dancing teachers to marriage announcements between members of the crew, particularly between those who were known not to like each other. Thus a man named Barthold, who had recently been given extra duty for a row with a bachelor named Schwarz, was announced as having married the latter's divorced wife, by this punishment smoothing over the feud; while two old cooks, who were noted for never working amicably on the same watch, were featured together as having baked the Barthold-Schwarz wedding cake. When one knew the real facts in the lives of the particular men, these announcements gave keen delight.

The whole newspaper was so small that I had soon read it through. Then my thoughts once more turned back to my diary and I began to write.

We had been on the sea just one month this day, and though we had accomplished much we had not yet captured a single ship. It seemed unbelievable that we could have been away so long. So busy had we been, the days had slipped away as if by magic.

I dropped my diary and began writing a letter to my mother, which I knew I might never be able to send, and which if sent might never reach its destination. Yet for some reason the impulse to write was too strong to be repressed. As I look back on these pages, I cannot help reflecting how impossible it is to foresee the future. This letter I later bore with me to my home in Poland, but the beloved eyes it was intended to reach were closed in death.

I was thus writing when suddenly at about ten o'clock I was roused by the peal of the ship's gong and the voice of the bugle and roll of the drum sounding "Clear for action!" I dropped my pen and seizing my cap hurried to station on the promenade deck. A steamer had been sighted.

At this point I have to mention that "Clear for action" meant that everybody had to rush to his station and await orders from the commandant's bridge.

In a few minutes all men were at their places. The ship's guard lay sprawled upon mattresses on the starboard deck, rifles in hand; above on the middle bridge the machine gun was planted ready for action, while at their stations starboard and port the gun crew loaded and trained their weapons.

I looked through my glasses at the sighted vessel. She was a single-funnelled steamer of fair proportions, evidently a good prize. As yet, however, she was too far away to be identified. We bore swiftly down, so that in a short time we were able to make out the markings of a German ship. This was both a relief and a disappointment to the officers, but especially to the crew which was already joyous in expectation of a capture. The vessel proved to be the fair ship *Asuncion* of Hamburg. Her captain later told us that he had at once recognized the *Kronprinz Wilhelm* but had been afraid to use his wireless lest his message betray his position to some British war vessel, many of which were in these waters.

On second thought we were overjoyed to meet the *Asuncion*. Already Commander Thierfelder was congratulating himself upon being able to resupply the *Kronprinz Wilhelm* with coal and provisions, of which we were in need, when to his disappointment he was told by the captain of the *Asuncion* that most of his stores had already been given to the S. M. S. *Karlsruhe*. All he could sparingly offer was a few chickens, some bottled beer, a little soap, tobacco, and some cigarettes. Our boats dolefully brought back these meagre supplies, thankful not to be asked for provisions ourselves.

The captain of the *Asuncion* also brought news that our old friend, the S. M. S. *Karlsruhe,* had captured an English steamer carrying six thousand tons of coal, and in addition to the officers of this vessel had on board as prisoners of war the officers and crew of an English ore-bearing steamer, sunk a short time before. The crews of these vessels the *Karlsruhe* intended sending on shore at the earliest opportunity.

Commander Thierfelder now called in Lieutenant Brinkmann, who showed the captain of the *Asuncion* his chart of the probable positions of enemy ships around us and talked over the best course which the *Asuncion* could follow to get away in safety. The commander then exchanged a friendly good-bye with the captain, and the latter put over our side for his own ship.

Our commander was now in a great hurry to get away. He wanted to steer for the *Karlsruhe* at once to obtain if possible some of her captured coal, for our supply was already running short. In fact, so much coal had been used during the last week that only a little over three days' running supply remained in our bunkers. This was a serious situation. For a whole month we had been cruising about without taking a single ship, and now within three days it was absolutely necessary that we capture a steamship from which we might coal—unless, by a happy

The INDIAN PRINCE, a British freight and passenger liner. It was the first ship to be sunk by the KRONPRINZ WILHELM and one of the latter's most valuable victims.

chance, we should overtake the *Karlsruhe* and get a supply of fuel from her.

Commander Thierfelder therefore gave the order to steam on. In courtesy to the *Asuncion* our band assembled on the forecastle head and struck up a lively piece, while our men, who had climbed to the tops of our masts and smokestacks or were lining the rails, gave a long cheer and a *Kaiserhoch!* to the friendly vessel. These were answered by the crew of the *Asuncion,* and we sped away on our separate voyages.

The *Asuncion,* we later learned, reached a South American port in safety, and there she gave a glowing account of our welfare.

We were now on the track of the *Karlsruhe.* But trailing a vessel at sea in war time is more difficult than making a similar search in times of peace. Neither the *Karlsruhe* nor the *Kronprinz Wilhelm* wished to use its wireless, lest the enemy get a clue to our position. With respect to the *Karlsruhe's* position, furthermore, we could depend on only one thing—that it was constantly changing. Taking everything into consideration we had far greater chance of missing than of meeting the cruiser. Nevertheless, the emergency was such that we had no choice, so we resolutely set out, basing our course upon the information given by the *Asuncion.* One thing of great aid in such a search should be mentioned. It was the negative information which we gathered from the position of enemy ships as given by Lieutenant Brinkmann. Where these ships were the *Karlsruhe* would not be, or if she was, she would be either in chase or in battle, in either of which cases we would not want to meet her. Our search must be where these ships were not. Brinkmann's charts accordingly became our guide.

That whole day and night we steamed rapidly ahead keeping a lookout for smoke or other signs of a ship. The next day dawned and passed and still no trace of friend or enemy. Another day at this rate and our coal would be gone. There would then be only one more move to make— to send out a call in code for aid and then wait, helpless, to be either rescued by a friend or discovered by the enemy— in which case we would scuttle the ship. Commander Thierfelder was resolved we should not be captured so long as there was a seacock in the bottom of the *Kronprinz Wilhelm* to be opened.

When night fell our watch was redoubled, for it was at night that the quickest surprises could take place. By day the smoke of friend or enemy was visible over the horizon before the ship itself, and we had time to keep ourselves hidden or to get away. By night under certain weather conditions, on the contrary, it was even possible to collide with an enemy without lights before seeing her. By day, also, the *Karlsruhe* would immediately be identified; by night a fatal mistake might be made.

Night was also dangerous in another way. Toward morning, while it was still dark, it was always possible to run near another ship which, though too far away to be seen, would yet at break of day be within the horizon. In such case, as light dawned, we would be confronted with an enemy who might at once open fire or give chase. However, the other ship might prove to be a merchantman or passenger liner, in which case at break of day we ourselves would be the gainers. It was this gamble upon what would be the story of the sea at daybreak that roused such suspense and made the diurnal lifting of night so exciting. In fact, except when we were actually capturing or being pursued by an enemy, daybreak was our most nerve-straining time.

The night of the fourth of September was a particularly dark one. At nine o'clock, as I was just getting ready to turn in, Hoffmann, who had been at my side, called my attention to a spot on the horizon.

"Niezy," he cried, "there's a light!"

At the instant he spoke the ship's lookout bell sounded and I rang the gong. At once the bugle began to call to station and the drum rolled as if to wake the dead. For the lights of a large steamer had appeared on the starboard horizon.

Instantly, all was in motion. The men, conscious of the ship's perilous condition for lack of fuel, ready for any action that might rescue us from it, leaped to their places and stood ready for the event. In the dark I could hear them speak to each other under their breath as they adjusted their bodies to their sprawled positions, some laughing in their excitement, others swearing, each after his own fashion giving vent to the excitement.

Soon we had come fairly near our prize, whose proportions were at least plainly discernible. As, however, we were running in complete darkness, we felt that we ourselves were not seen. The questions which each man was asking himself were: Is the prize armed?—If so, how heavily?—Will she give battle?

At a distance of about five hundred yards our rockets went up, displaying under their glare a large single-funnelled British freight and passenger liner, the *Indian Prince*—from every sign an exceptional prize.

The enemy, contrary to our expectations, seemed not to be worried over our approach, evidently sure we were a vessel of her own nationality. Not until Commander Thierfelder signalled to the ship to surrender and follow us did she note her error. We now saw that it was fortunate for us we had been able to creep up on this vessel, for she proved to be a fast steamer and might, if warned in time, have put out her lights and escaped in the darkness, just as we on a previous occasion had ourselves slipped away from a fast British cruiser. There was nothing now for her to do but haul down her colours and steam on ahead of us.

All night the steamer sped on directly in front of us. Commander Thierfelder had ordered the vessel's captain to extinguish all his lights, and our men aloft kept a sharp lookout lest our prize display secret lights or signals. Meanwhile, the gun crews were kept at their posts for instant action.

The captain of the *Indian Prince,* however, recognized the hopelessness of his position and showed good judgment in not attempting to deceive us. He told us afterward that he had some kegs of dynamite in his hold with fuses set, with which to blow the bottom out of his ship, but had neglected to use them in the hope that his vessel would be rescued before we could unload and sink her. He still jollily continued to hold to his hope even for some days after he had been a prisoner of war aboard our ship, until he at last heard the explosion of the boilers of his vessel as it went to the bottom. Then, as one of my friends who was with him at the time told me, he merely shrugged his shoulders and remarked dryly: "Your ship, the *Kronprinz Wilhelm*—it will sooner or later go to the bottom, too."

At six o'clock next morning all hands were piped to station. In fact, everyone had been up since daybreak to get a good look at the prize. The *Indian Prince* was a powerful vessel of extraordinary size, painted black except for her cabin and her forecastle head; these were white and there were a red band and three white ostrich plumes on her funnel.

The name *Indian Prince* gave all hands a feeling of good omen. The "Prince of India" was thus to be the first enemy ship sunk by the *Kronprinz Wilhelm*. Our crew saw in this a prognostication of the fall of India—the beginning of the dismemberment of the British Empire. Though the omen was far-fetched, yet in times like these men catch at straws; and a crew upon a forlorn hope, as was this of the *Kronprinz Wilhelm,* has its superstitions easily aroused. I heard seamen talking of the sinking of the *Indian Prince* as if it were really India itself which was going to the bottom.

For my part I could not share these emotions. A ship has always appeared to me like a living being. To destroy it seems like murder. I looked with a feeling of distress upon the doomed vessel to think that this splendid piece of machinery, this representative of the triumph of the mind of man over nature, must soon be but a heap of scrap iron a mile below the surface of the sea.

As all hands took their stations, Commander Thierfelder signalled to the *Indian Prince* to come alongside. Ten minutes later the vessel had reached our port and was made fast.

Our manner of bringing the vessel alongside was unique and the same in all cases. Instead of coming to a standstill while the other vessel slowly steamed to our side, the *Kronprinz Wilhelm* slowed down to two miles an hour and continued to maintain this speed. The second vessel now came abreast of us some hundred yards away. Then both ships, still maintaining an equal speed of two knots, gradually converged upon each other. When our bows neared each other two six-inch cables were passed across them and two across our poops, a man being stationed at each

cable, ax in hand, to cut loose in case of need. The speed
of two knots was now maintained as long as the vessels
remained side by side. This method of lying by while keeping up speed had this advantage: if a second prize or an
enemy cruiser should suddenly appear we had but a few
cables to pull in or chop in two, had steam and momentum
up on both vessels, and could speed away on the instant in
separate directions as we had done in the case of the surprise attack while we were alongside the S. M. S. *Karlsruhe*.

The captain of the *Indian Prince,* who now came aboard
us, reported that his vessel, which was of the Princess Line
of London and Newcastle, carried a cargo of cocoa, coffee,
and some provisions. As passengers he had on board three
German-Americans and twelve Africans. His ship proved
a most precious prize—one of the most valuable, in fact,
of all we took on the voyage.

While the captain of the *Indian Prince* was thus giving
a description of his cargo, we sent men aboard to carry off
the ship's charts and compass, together with all other
navigating instruments, so that, should we suddenly be
forced to leave the vessel's side, the *Indian Prince* would
not be able to orientate herself to get away.

Commander Thierfelder would now gladly have begun
coaling from the bunkers of his prize, but we were in too
dangerous waters. Hourly our wireless gave us news of
the vicinity of new battleships. It behooved us to move
on until we should reach a more quiet spot. The captain

of our prize was accordingly sent back to his vessel with orders to follow us.

While we were thus steaming along slowly so as not to use too much coal, war news of great importance came by wireless. Our crew was jubilant to learn that five English cruisers had been sunk by German submarines and torpedo boats, that fifty thousand French troops had crossed the Swiss border and been interned, that the French main army had been surrounded and with it an English auxiliary force of sixty thousand men, and that the Prussians had won a brilliant victory over the Russians at Tannenberg, taking one hundred and seventy-five thousand prisoners and wiping out as many more.

When this news was read to the men, they fairly went wild. It was the first good war news the crew had received. The men, already war-weary, saw in a flash the end of the whole disagreeable business approaching. Soon, perhaps, they would be steaming home to see their folks again.

It is marvellous how easily men believe what they want to. For a short time I lost much in the estimation of my fellow officers for being pessimistic over a speedy ending of the war. They pointed to this wireless dispatch.

"Isn't that enough?" they asked.

I held my peace.

Hoffmann, who had renewed his bet with me about capturing a ship, now came up and claimed his box of cigars, which, since we had captured a vessel within his week, I owed him. I accordingly went to the ship's store, bought him a box of Havanas, and had the amount checked off against my pay. Then we renewed the bet for the next week, "Aunt Hoffmann," as we playfully called my friend because of his punctilious habits, maintaining that we would capture a second vessel within seven days. These bets, of course, were of no consequence to the fate of the *Kronprinz Wilhelm* or her victims, but they gave us so much diversion that I must mention them.

At morning mess, for instance, Hoffmann, who sat opposite me, never took his seat without chirping cheerfully: "Well, Niezy, to-day I'm going to win that box of cigars."

And when we sat down to evening mess he likewise remarked: "Well, Niezy, to-night I'm going to win that box of cigars."

This he continued until Brinkmann, who sat next him, dubbed him "Cigar-box Hoffmann," which won the classic retort: *"Lausch-Wind Brinkmann"*—Listen-to-the-wind Brinkmann—in reference to the wireless expert's profession. Ever after that, in times of good humour, Brinkmann would suddenly call over to Hoffmann: "Say, old Cigar Box, hand me the plate of biscuits."

Whereupon the other would retort: "All right, Listen-to-the-wind—and pass them back again."

On the morning after the capture of the *Indian Prince,* as Hoffmann came down late to the table, all hands rose in concert and bowed with formal courtesy. Hoffmann, who did not know what the ceremony was about, looked

dubiously from one to the other of us until Lieutenant
Biermann at the other end of the table solemnly pledged:
"*Hoch* to the gallant conqueror of—the box of cigars!"

Diversions such as these relieved the strenuous work
which made up our day. Since the capture of the *Indian
Prince* the seriousness of our mood, for the moment
relieved by the capture, had even increased. The men looked
upon themselves and their ship as heightened in value
since capturing the precious prize, and from lowest to
highest they felt the added importance.

All night Saturday, the fifth of September, we lay quiet
upon the sea in order to save coal—our prize, a hundred
yards astern, likewise resting upon the gentle swells while
her engines remained at peace. Next day everybody expected to be busy coaling. As Sunday dawned, however,
the position of our vessels was still too perilous; the command was therefore given, "Slow speed ahead," and on
we steamed leisurely, burning a minimum of coal.

Our fuel was holding out better than we had expected.
As we had been averaging about ten miles an hour, the most
economical speed for the *Kronprinz Wilhelm,* we had
burned only half the amount expected. At this rate we still
had three days' fuel on hand. In case of emergency, however, this was but a meagre supply, which made me
wonder whether Commander Thierfelder was not taking
undue risks by not beginning to coal at once. He knew
better than I how dangerous the waters about us were, and
felt that he was taking less risk in avoiding being sighted

than in having on board the means of flight if discovered.

While we thus cruised along, our men were not idle. Some were getting ready our coaling tackle, while others were busy taking measures to receive the passengers and crew of the *Indian Prince*. The former were to be treated as if they were our own passengers, given first-class berths, with the freedom of a part of the first-class promenade deck for exercise, while the first-class library was set aside as their dining hall. The officers and crew, now prisoners of war, were to receive second-class quarters, where a guard would be posted.

This Sunday morning, as on the day before, news again came by wireless that the war situation was most favourable for the Central Powers. German troops stood before Paris; fifteen fliers had bombed the city. That afternoon, after all hands had been assembled on the stern deck and addressed by the commander, the band played and the men were given ten cigarettes apiece with a bottle of beer for each two. All were in the best of humour. The outlook seemed splendid beyond belief.

On Monday passengers and crew of the *Indian Prince* were transferred to their respective quarters on our vessel. There was a total absence of grumbling as the men came aboard, dragging their baggage or bearing it upon their shoulders. The passengers accepted our courtesies with thanks—indeed they were gratified to be treated as free men and given first-class berths—while officers and crew, bowing to the lot of war, took their second-class quarters, glad not to be given worse. One man told us later that a rumour had gone round among the crew of the *Indian Prince* that they were all to be shot at sundown. Needless to say, this rumour was unfounded. They were all given as comfortable pillows on which to lay their heads and as good food with which to warm their blood as any man aboard the *Kronprinz Wilhelm* received.

On Tuesday, the eighth, the *Indian Prince* was laid along our port and at 2 P. M. coaling began. Some of our crew were at the same time detailed to bring over to our decks all machinery, tackle, cordage, and furniture which could possibly be of use to us on our voyage. This work went on all afternoon and night, while at the same time coaling steadily progressed. At nine o'clock Wednesday morning the bunkers of the *Indian Prince* were empty, all valuable stores and machinery having been taken from her. At ten o'clock we drew in our cable and steamed off to starboard, leaving on board the doomed vessel an officer and four men with a boat in which to make back to our side. These men were to open the seacocks of the fated ship.

In the side of every vessel somewhat below the water line is a large circular manhole two or more feet in diameter into which fits a steel plate or plug. The plate is fastened to the reinforced sides of the ship by means of bolts arranged at intervals of a few inches around the circumference of the hole. Into this plate fit large pipes which, communicating with the sea, form an intake for salt water.

This plug and its manhole are together called the ship's seacocks.

Opening a ship's seacocks is a feat of not a little skill and danger. The nuts of the bolts which fasten the plate to its manhole must be unscrewed in such manner that the plate comes loose suddenly and not gradually, so that the sailor who opens it may work until the last minute and then escape from the inrushing water. To do this special strategy is necessary.

The men of the *Kronprinz Wilhelm* went about the operation in the following way: The day after the *Indian Prince* was captured some men were sent down into her hold to begin preliminary work upon the seacocks. Two of these men carefully unscrewed one rusty nut at a time, thoroughly greased its threads, and then screwed it back into place again before loosening the next. While this was being done, the other men unbolted the pipes leading into the seacock and removed all obstructions in the way of hasty escape from its neighbourhood.

This preliminary work of greasing and loosening was done merely that the seacocks might be in readiness for immediate opening without loss of time should an enemy appear or other emergency require hasty action. The seacocks thus greased and disencumbered of pipes and impedimenta were then left in place, and the men returned to our decks.

It was these two men who were now again sent aboard the fated ship to finish the opening of her seacocks. The officer and his men stood on deck at the hatch, while one strong fellow, a man named Fitzmüller, who made a specialty of this work, climbed down to the seacock, equipped with a monkey wrench and a sledge hammer. Around his waist was tied a rope, the other end of which was held by the men above for use in emergency.

Fitzmüller, under direction of the officer above, took off the nuts from every second bolt in the circle. Being recently loosened and greased, they came off easily. After he had thus gone completely around the circumference of the plate, the plug was being held to the ship by only half its former number of bolts. Beginning once more, the adroit seaman again removed every second nut from the remaining bolts. The plate was now held by only one fourth the original number of bolts. This process of halving was continued until the plug was finally being held by only two bolts on diametrically opposite sides of the circumference of the seacock. By this time the pressure of the water on the outside was meeting with so little resistance that the plate was bending slightly inward, letting water spurt between the rubber packing and the steel plate up into the hold.

Fitzmüller, sweating at every pore, now thrust his wrench into his overalls pocket, picked up his sledge, and called out: "Ready!"

At this signal the men on deck took in the slack of the rope, so that if necessary they could hoist their imperilled comrade up out of danger.

Fitzmüller now lifted his sledge hammer, took accurate aim, and with a single vigorous blow mashed one of the two protruding bolts through its nut and hole. As the plate did not fly loose he let the heavy hammer fall again, throwing all his strength into the blow, this time upon the remaining bolt. With a dull explosion the whole two-foot plate flew loose, and a geyser of sea water gushed upward into the hold.

Fitzmüller at once leaped for the ladder and, still holding to the sledge, clambered up to safety. Had he slipped or been washed away by the force of the water, his comrades on deck would have fished him up by means of the rope.

By this time the ship was rapidly filling. As the doors through all compartments had previously been opened, the water coming through this one seacock at once began flowing to all parts of the hold. The men on deck were now in real danger, for a sudden listing of the vessel or its unexpectedly rapid sinking might mean their death. All, therefore, at once scrambled over the side into their boat, the officer jumping in last of all, and pulled away as fast as possible lest they be sucked into the vortex of the sinking ship.

For a short space the *Indian Prince* settled rapidly, giving us reason to expect her to go to the bottom within half an hour. Our expectations, however, were not realized, for the ship soon began to rest at the same level. Air had doubtless lodged in the tops of compartments and been imprisoned in bunkers, so that though the ship must ultimately go down no one could foretell how long the sinking would take.

Accordingly, as we were in a hurry to get away from the spot, at 1 P. M. Commander Thierfelder sent over some men to blast a hole in the vessel's side. Dynamite was placed at the base of the ship's two masts and amidships, and the fuses lit, after which our men rowed swiftly away. Hardly had they reached our side when three crashes, one hard upon the other, shattered the side and decks of the vessel, and the *Indian Prince* began to sink rapidly. First, her bows filled; then the gigantic steamer stood perpendicularly on her prow like a tower rising from the ocean and slid with a rush out of sight.

At the instant her funnel plunged under, a tremendous explosion of her boilers took place, throwing a cloud of steam and water high into the air. An instant later only a vortex of tossing, oily water gave evidence that a great steamer had gone to the bottom.

"This is war," I thought as I snapped my camera. "An hour ago this splendid ship might have been of great service to mankind. Now she is no more."

The men of the *Kronprinz Wilhelm* took a different view. This great vessel, they argued, might soon have been used to carry to the enemy ammunition with which to shoot down their brothers in the trenches. All is in the point of view.

After the *Indian Prince* had gone to her eternal locker,

we steamed over the spot to fish up any stray bits of wreckage which might be floating about. Finding none, we put on speed again to the northwest. The first great prize had been caught and dispatched. The *Kronprinz Wilhelm* was off in search of the next.

Chapter VII

FRIENDS, HO!

ON FRIDAY, the eleventh of September, shortly after daybreak, a single smokestack appeared over the horizon. I was asleep at the time, but the din of the ship's bugle, gong, and drum would have waked the dead. Getting hastily into my uniform I stumbled half awake to my station on the promenade deck, when just as I was adjusting myself to the emergency of action the order "At ease!" came down.

The steamer sighted was the *Ebernburg* of Bremen, which Commander Thierfelder had been advised he should meet in these waters.

The *Ebernburg* had no sooner come up, however, than, instead of stopping to take her alongside, the *Kronprinz Wilhelm* increased her speed, exchanging signals with the other vessel as she steamed along. The neighbourhood, in short, was too hot with Allied warships to permit us to stop. The *Ebernburg* accordingly took up her position in our wake, while we steamed on in search of a safe coaling place.

Next day, however, after an all-night steam, the *Ebernburg* came upon our port and made fast. We were in a favourable place for coaling and the weather was as calm as could be desired.

The crew of the *Ebernburg* now showed the greatest eagerness to come aboard our ship and meet our men. They had heard much of the doings of the *Kronprinz Wilhelm*— most of it exaggeration, of course, since we had as yet only begun our adventurous career—and were much disappointed to learn that we had sunk only one large steamer, as seven had already been credited to us by the magnifying voice of rumour. But one was one, they said, glad that that one was a large one.

We now began taking on coal, provisions, and especially one thousand tons of fresh water of which we were in great need. For, although we had large condensers aboard for condensing our own fresh water from the salt, water thus manufactured is disproportionately expensive and is cordially detested by the crew because of its insipid taste. Even rain water that has lain in casks for an indefinite period tastes better than freshly condensed sea water which, as a seaman once expressed it, "tastes like the beer they brew in hell."

To lend variety to the monotony of coaling, our commander now struck upon a whimsical expedient—one, however, which won him heightened regard with his officers and renewed popularity with the crew. The ship's band, in brief, was ordered to play martial tunes at the three coaling stations, alternately playing fore, centre, and aft. This made the coaling tars work with spirit, lending the zest of an heroic atmosphere to the operation. There is nothing like music for raising the spirits of men. As in the army the saying goes, "A singing army is a conquering army"—so with us aboard ship, "A singing crew is an invincible crew." It was inspiring to see the men in their grimy coaling trousers, which sometimes looked for all the world like nothing more than thin diapers, swinging their shovels and swaying their forms to patriotic tunes, now humming along with the air, now working in silence. And they shovelled half again as much coal than if they had worked without the music.

Our band seemed to enjoy the sport of playing to the coalers, especially as it was always greeted with cheers by the favoured crew whenever it made its change of place.

There were three musical groups on board our ship—a brass band, a stringed orchestra, and a junior band consisting of nonprofessionals.

The brass band, having the loudest instruments, played at the coaling stations, the ten men who composed it being all professional players.

The orchestra at this time consisted of seven men under the leadership of a musician named Weber. There were a first and a second violin, a bass viol, a cornet, a trombone, a drum, cymbals, and a piano. The musicians were all elderly men, not so fit for naval or seaman's duty, but exceptionally well qualified as musicians.

Weber was regarded by us all as a genius. In person not very tall, but well proportioned, with long black hair, a

Roman nose, and coal-black eyes, he looked the part. He had studied at various famous conservatories, could play any instrument with the skill of a professional, and was especially versatile as a composer. At about this time he composed in honour of the ship the "Kronprinz Wilhelm March," a piece which the men liked and would whistle in their leisure hours. Later he composed a "Prinz Eitel Friedrich March" in honour of the ship of that name. This song became equally popular with our own.

Toward me Weber was particularly friendly, perhaps for a good reason. For among the other honours laid upon me had been the duty of being officer of the bands. My work in this connection was to look to the welfare of the various members, hear and settle their complaints, make their engagements; that is, order them to appear at such and such times on such and such occasions—in short, be their official guardian and representative aboard ship. I think that Commander Thierfelder gave me this position in token of my fond weakness for telling of the operas I had heard in different parts of the world.

Weber, knowing me to be a Pole, often played Polish pieces or the Polish national anthem, "Boże cos´ Polskę," to flatter me. In return I did him good turns whenever an opportunity offered, so that we contracted a lasting friendship for each other.

Weber was at first very glad to have his band detailed to play while the men coaled, welcoming the practice it gave his men. In the course of time, however, I am afraid he had cause to rue the expedient. The weather was usually hot, the sea calm, and under such conditions making music is nothing more than a polite form of torture. I often noticed that the tune lagged wearily despite Weber's efforts to bolster it up.

That Saturday afternoon of the twelfth of September, while we were thus musically coaling from the *Ebernburg,* a lively scene took place below decks in the second-class staterooms where our prisoners of war from the *Indian Prince* were being held. At noon Commander Thierfelder had sent down Lieutenant Fix with some officers to ask the captive English officers to sign a statement that, if put aboard another vessel and soon afterward set at liberty, they would not again take up arms against Germany or in any manner help in the present struggle against her. This was the customary statement signed by officers, prisoners of war, under similar circumstances.

The English officers, however, indignantly refused to sign, becoming offensive when the matter was pressed, so that had they not been prisoners of war and had not Lieutenant Fix and his aides been under naval orders, a scuffle would have taken place on the spot. Fix, however, calmly told the men that if they signed the paper they would have liberty and a chance to fight again in future wars, but that if they did not sign they would still have no chance to fight in the present struggle, as they would be kept aboard the *Kronprinz Wilhelm* until the last; and, since the ship would be scuttled rather than surrendered, they would very likely only go down with her in the end. As this logic did not seem to impress them, our officers came back, reasoning that if the men chewed long enough upon the matter they would not fail to sign in the end.

The news of the "fierce objections" of the Englishmen was soon spread about the ship by a certain sailor named Scholke, an ex-buffoon and professional comedian, who was one of the guards detailed to stand post in the prisoners' quarters. Scholke mimicked the words and actions of the excited English officers with such success that he gathered a crowd, drawing down a chorus of guffaws. The laughter quickly spread to the coaling shifts, almost disrupting the operations, the appearance of officers alone preventing damage to the ship's morale.

To fill the measure of the day's experiences, some of our men who were off duty began fishing for sharks, signs of which had not been wanting for some days past, and three large man-eaters were caught. Of this sport, in which the crew indulged more as time went on, I shall say more later.

For a few days past we had been expecting the approach of the German steamer *Prussia,* which would bring us a further supply of coal. On Monday afternoon, as we were coaling from the *Ebernburg,* the *Prussia* at last put in her appearance. As this friendly vessel steamed up, it looked for all the world as if a German naval base were being established here in mid-ocean. The three large ships, lying near each other in the middle of the sea, by contrast with the limitless expanse of surrounding ocean, looked like a little village on a horizon-bounded desert.

The captain of the *Prussia* soon came over to us and a brief conversation took place, in the midst of which Brinkmann's voice sounded through the speaking tube: "S O S from the *Cape Trafalgar*. *Cape Trafalgar* engaged by British cruiser *Carmania*. Longitude 35 degrees west, latitude 26 degrees south. Steaming N. N. W."

A minute later: *"Cape Trafalgar* on fire. S O S repeated."

At the first message Commander Thierfelder commanded the *Ebernburg* to let go our side. Then he telegraphed "All ready" to the engine room.

The *Cape Trafalgar,* Commander Thierfelder knew, was only an auxiliary cruiser—no match for the *Carmania.*

"I'm going to her," he said, turning to the captain of the *Prussia.* "In the meantime steam north three hours at twelve knots. Then come back here and wait for us."

As the captain of the *Prussia* went over our side, identical orders were given to the captain of the *Ebernburg.* This done, Commander Thierfelder telegraphed "Full speed ahead!" and as our speed picked up put the helm about in the direction of the island of Trinidad, where the engagement between the *Cape Trafalgar* and the *Carmania* was taking place.

As we rushed along at our utmost speed, the *Kronprinz Wilhelm* became a scene of rapid preparations. The gong had sounded, and all hands were at their respective stations. The ship's guard lay sprawled upon its mattresses, the gun crews stood at their weapons, while the ammunition train brought shell upon deck from the magazine. In the hospital room stretchers were got ready, bandages unrolled, and instruments uncased. Everything was put in readiness for action to a finish.

Meanwhile, Lieutenant Brinkmann was calling down the S O S of the *Cape Trafalg*ar as rapidly as it came, giving renewed details.

"*Cape Trafalgar* on fire and sinking. *Carmania* also on fire."

For a time the *Cape Trafalgar's* call for help continued uninterruptedly; then after about fifteen minutes it ceased. We sent out repeated calls for answer but, receiving none, inferred that the *Cape Trafalgar* had gone down.

Our own situation had now become critical. There were doubtless in the neighbourhood into which we were speeding many Allied war vessels. All of them must have heard the calls of the *Cape Trafalgar,* which, though in German code, had been supplemented by the *Carmania* in the British code. These warships would now be speeding to the same spot. If we arrived we would be too late to assist the German vessel which we already regarded as sunk, and would most probably be just in time to become engaged ourselves. We had, in addition, let the whole sea about us know of our presence by answering the calls of the *Cape Trafalgar.* A concerted search would therefore doubtless be made for us in the neighbourhood into which we were speeding. Commander Thierfelder put the *Kronprinz Wilhelm* about and steamed back full speed in the direction whence we had come.

We learned later that the *Cape Trafalgar* had been sunk with the loss of many lives, while the *Carmania* had been set on fire and so badly damaged that she was forced to run into Pernambuco to avoid sinking. It was a case of two vessels unevenly matched fighting to a finish.

The news of the sinking of the *Cape Trafalgar* depressed our men. Some of them had friends aboard the sunken ship, whom they mourned as lost. Others became angry that the *Cape Trafalgar* should be defeated, despite her inferior armament. They were of course glad to hear that the *Carmania* had been badly handled in the engagement.

I had a friend aboard the *Cape Trafalgar,* an engineer named Powell, who by the queerest stroke of luck was saved. A shell from the *Carmania* blew a hole in the side of the *Cape Trafalgar* amidships above the water line some twenty feet from him. As he in a dazed condition involuntarily lurched toward the spot, he was thrown out into the sea by a blast of air compressed by another explosion somewhere else in the hold. He was uninjured, however, swam about for an hour, and was finally picked up by a small boat.

He wrote to me two years later that he had never before in his life known that he could be afraid of anything. But as he swam about in the hot waters of the tropical ocean the dread of sharks, which might at any instant dash up and bite him in two, almost turned his mind. He said that he prayed every minute he swam, and when picked up was speechless for an hour. Anyone who knows the iron-willed Powell will appreciate the effect the thought of a shark's bite can have on a man.

Soon after the *Kronprinz Wilhelm* turned about from the *Cape Trafalgar* chase, night set in; so, in order to save coal and not run into danger, Commander Thierfelder stopped our engines. We thus lay quiet all night; then picked up our speed again at five thirty in the morning, and sped on toward our rendezvous, where we found the *Ebernburg* and the *Prussia* already arrived, waiting for us.

We at once brought the *Ebernburg* alongside and continued our interrupted coaling, which went on without intermission until nightfall; then we again stood off from the collier. Next morning as we were laying the *Ebernburg* alongside again, the single-funnelled steamer *Pontos* of Hamburg came in sight.

When this vessel had steamed up, our coaling spot indeed began to look like a naval base. We now had around us three large merchantmen, the *Prussia,* the *Ebernburg,* and the *Pontos*—all laden with supplies and fuel. The *Pontos* brought us a heavy cargo of coal. But as we had not finished coaling from the *Ebernburg* and had not even touched the supply of the *Prussia,* Commander Thierfelder ordered the *Pontos* to steam out of sight to the northwest and do scout duty, while we continued coaling from the *Ebernburg.*

Toward five o'clock that evening five passengers from the *Indian Prince* were transferred from their commodious quarters on our ship to the cabins of the *Ebernburg,* which would soon be unloaded and ready for departure. Next day coaling from the vessel was completed. The Africans and the crew of the *Indian Prince* were then sent aboard the *Ebernburg,* together with three of our own crew, who had meanwhile fallen too sick for further service. The *Ebernburg* then stood off at a convenient distance to await further orders.

At dawn the following day the *Prussia* lay by on our port and gave us eight hundred tons of coal in the course of the day. We were now beginning to settle down into a port-and-harbour atmosphere—taking on coals, water, and provisions, all hands being as busy as the pressure of work could make them. All that would be necessary to bring excitement to this routine was the sight of an enemy vessel.

At six that evening the treat came. The gong and bugle sounded "Clear for action!" A sail was on the horizon.

At once the *Prussia* let go our sides, and we steamed with a speed of eighteen miles upon the stranger, reaching her at 7 P. M. As she did not show a flag, our port gun fired a blank shot which caused the ship to put into the wind, whereupon our prize crew immediately got into its boat and rowed over.

What was the men's surprise, however, when on nearing the side of the vessel they beheld the captain of the sailing ship *Macdiarmic* of Genoa leisurely sitting upon a stool

near the rail scraping a fiddle, while a sailor, who sat
beside him and from a distance seemed to be biting on the
end of a rope as if to loosen a knot, was tooting shrilly
upon a flute. The wind had been blowing away from our
men so that they had not heard the music. The rest of the
Macdiarmic's crew sat about the rail looking with curiosity
upon our prize boat and its mother ship, yet at the same
time keeping a vigilant eye upon their fiddling captain.

At last, as the prize boat came alongside, the captain of
the *Macdiarmic* got off his stool, gave his fiddle to the
player of the flute, who was the first mate, and deigned
to ask in a musical Italian voice: "What's the matter?"

Our officer explained his mission, whereupon the Italian
blandly and condescendingly smiled.

"The *Macdiarmic* is an Italian ship," he said in tones
which marked him as a cultured man. "She is bound from
Hamburg by way of the Azores with a neutral cargo."

Hereupon he sent one of his sailors after his ship's
papers. These proved that he spoke the truth, so that our
boat was forced to leave the neutral vessel unmolested.

As the prize crew began rowing back the *Macdiarmic*
wanted to put herself before the wind again, but Commander Thierfelder ordered her to halt. At 8 P. M., however, the ship was finally allowed to proceed and was soon
lost in the darkness. The last our men remember of her
was the spectacle of the majority of her crew still lining
the rail just before dark, while the figures of her captain
and his accompanist retook their places, the one with his

fiddle, the other with his flute, to all appearances continuing their interrupted vesper duet.

This idyllic scene upon mid-ocean in the very heat of a great war made a deep impression upon some of our men when the prize crew told of it. Scholke, our comedian, who seemed always to be in a position where he could see everything, happened to be a member of this prize crew. Next morning he borrowed a violin bow from our bandmaster, put a stick with a pair of trousers wrapped round it under his chin to represent a violin, sat upon the ship's rail, and by pretending to play and then getting down slowly to say: "What's the matter?" et cetera, brought forth roars of laughter from a willing audience.

Next morning was Sunday, but coaling from the *Prussia* continued. After breakfast an orderly came to Commander Thierfelder from the prisoners' quarters to report that the English officers had decided to sign the agreement.

Now, naval officers recognize each other the world over as men of honour and trust each other's word. Rather than break their word, solemnly given as officers, they will usually suffer more than for any other cause.

Lieutenant Fix was accordingly sent down to the prisoners. The English officers gathered round their captain, reread the paper which Fix presented, then, after their captain had signed, added their names in silence. This done they were told that they were free passengers and were at once sent over to the *Prussia*.

At about the same time the *Prussia* sent some of her crew to take service with us to replace the sick men to fill new positions created by the emergency. These men had already visited us the day before, knew our crew, and were quickly at home.

In the next general gathering of our crew some of these men gave us an account of their experiences since the declaration of war, amusing us much by their description of the terror which the name *Kronprinz Wilhelm* had created in South American shipping circles. Some companies, they said, had refused to let their ships go out of port until they should get word that the *Kronprinz Wilhelm* had been captured or sunk. This delighted our crew beyond measure and brought down extended cheers.

Coaling from the *Prussia* continued all day despite the Sabbath. There was reason for haste, and self-preservation is the first law of the sea. At 5 P. M. the merchantman let go our port. Our band played a farewell piece, a threefold "Hurrah!" rose from our crew, and the *Prussia* steamed rapidly away. At seven o'clock we had gotten up speed and, overtaking the vessel, again our crew gave three cheers which were at once answered by her crew and echoed by the crew of the *Pontos* which was steaming behind us. Our band now played "Es braust ein Ruf wie Donnerhall," and as a finale "Muss ich denn, muss ich denn, zum Städtchen hinaus." Then we sped past our friend and soon lost her from sight.

The sea had by this time become too rough for coaling, so next day the *Pontos* steamed along in our wake, awaiting a settling of the wind.

Coaling at sea in time of peace is no simple operation; in time of war it becomes increasingly complex. First, we had to take into account that at any moment the enemy might appear. Our ship must be ready at the sound of the bugle to let go and speed away. Second, there were usually enemy prisoners on board whom we hoped to send ashore at the earliest opportunity; these men must by no means witness the operation of coaling, lest facts of military importance reach the enemy. Then, it was necessary that we always coal on the same side of the ship; when the sea was rough the vessels lying beside us constantly rubbed and plunged into our sides, as we into theirs, denting plates, opening seams, and ruining the appearance of the ship. Also the grime of coaling transformed a deck once so clean that supper might have been eaten off it into the semblance of a coal barge, sooty, dented, splintered, filthy. The crews of captured vessels must by no means see the ship in this condition. Our starboard side was therefore sacred ground, all coaling being done on the port. When we attacked a vessel, or approached a neutral, or came alongside a surrendered craft, we showed our starboard. The two sides of our ship soon became a kind of obverse and reverse. The starboard was painted, scrubbed, and polished; it shone and glittered in the sun; the port gradually became a lamentable wreck of sooty, dented, mangled iron, often

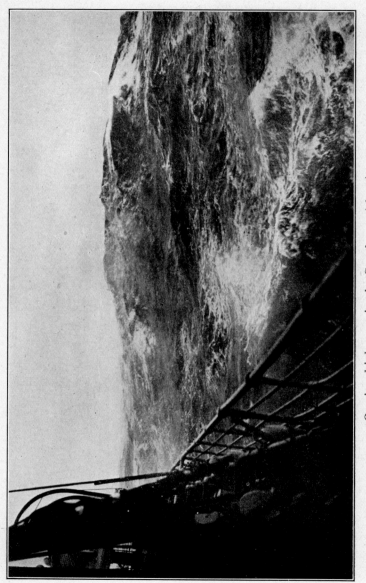

Cutting high seas in the Southern Atlantic

leaking so heavily through open seams that we had to keep all pumps going to prevent listing.

While thus waiting for the sea to calm, our crew was not idle. Repair work and painting had constantly to be done, and the men were put through their regular military drill.

When the men were called to military drill, each group hastened to its proper station. The officers of the guard instructed their men in the use and care of their weapons, in methods of attack and defence; the munition train went through the motions of bringing ammunition upon deck, while the hospital corps did all that would be its duty when in action. Each division thus went about its special work, the men rivalling each other in their zeal for praise or achievement.

Not quite so attractive and far from so enjoyable was the weekly duty of washing clothes. Monday, the twenty-first of September, being wash day all hands after the regular morning military drill assembled on the lee promenade deck with soap, scrubbing brushes, and water pails in hand, and began scrubbing the dirty laundry. The buckets were filled by letting them down into the sea at the end of a rope or by using the deck hose. The men usually soaked their trousers or shirts in the buckets, then laid them out flat upon deck, and began rubbing away. Often, however, they simply tied a rope around the clothes and let them dangle overboard into the water. As the ship sped along, the linen thus suspended plunged in and out of the water, churning and scrubbing itself. This "lazy-man's wash," however, had one disadvantage. The clothes thus suspended might be mistaken by dolphins or sharks for something edible and so suffer damage or be lost. A number of garments were thus bitten off on this voyage. Officers preferably sent their suits to the laundry.

The laundry, a suite of rooms on the lower deck aft, was presided over by seven dexterous Chinamen. These men knew their trade as only the Orientals do. They could transform a limp, disreputable-looking, coal-dirtied, sweat-pasted suit of clothes into a trimly starched white uniform as if by magic.

I had a great deal of fun with these Chinamen. When nothing else was on the programme, I would spend a half hour with them, asking them to translate a sentence into Chinese, repeating it after them until I had learned it. In return I amused myself by teaching them how to play chess, in which game, however, they seemed to make as little headway as I did with their language. They could always remember how to make a particular move but could not of their own initiative go on to the next.

Commander Thierfelder had a little trouble with the peaceful fellows trying to impress on them the seriousness of using too much fresh water in their washing. They did not like being put on water rations. At last the order came down that all laundry was to be rinsed with salt water only, and the Chinamen had to pocket their ire. This they did, swearing in Chinese, which did us no harm.

From Monday to Thursday, as the sea was so rough that coaling from the *Pontos* could not be thought of, our crew spent its time in military drill and cleaning ship. Then on Thursday afternoon Commander Thierfelder put the men through *Allemansmanöver*—All-men's Manœuvre.

Allemansmanöver was the same as "Clear for action!" except that no enemy was at hand. At three blasts of the bugle the men leaped to their stations and went through the motions of "Clear for action!" *Allemansmanöver* served to correlate the habitual motions learned in drill, so that when an enemy actually appeared our total crew worked as a unit, mechanically doing its manifold duties with no possibility of mistake. In fact, so habitual did these emergency duties become that after a time the first stages of "Clear for action!" might be gone through without the seaman's being fully roused from sleep. At the command "Clear for action!" or *Allemansmanöver,* he simply rolled or was spanked out of his hammock and sped to his place, waking up during the process. Through the instrumentality of *Allemansmanöver* the voyage was often made exciting in dull times and the crew kept in practice during a scarcity of prize ships.

To be sure, we were by no means free from monotony. An extended voyage at sea, even when made under as exciting conditions as ours, is more monotonous than it sounds when recounted afterward. In the account the dreary hours are passed over. In the actual experience, however, there are long intervals of monotonous routine.

Thus, on Friday, the twenty-fifth of September, as the sea had somewhat calmed down, we took the *Pontos* on our port and coaled all day. The *Pontos*, by the way, had originally carried a large supply of provisions, but meeting the ill-fated *Cape Trafalgar* had given away all her oxen and larger meat, so that the Trinidad sharks finally got it. She still had a supply of miscellaneous provisions, however. We received in addition to packed food, seven ducks, some chickens, and four wethers, all alive. By evening the sea had again become rough, and next day it was once more impossible to coal. On Sunday, however, we took advantage of a calmer sea, coaling until noon, when we again had to let go because of the driving swells.

Next day we had to clean ship. Like a soldiers' barracks, only larger and more complex, our vessel was divided into many quarters, to each one of which was detailed a certain number of the crew. Each detail cleaned its designated part. That day, after "policing" the vessel, the men were set to work making the special "uniforms" to be used when coaling. As all seamen are handy at making their own clothes and we had good instructors aboard, our men made quite presentable uniforms.

The word "uniform," however, may convey a wrong impression. The "coaling uniform" consisted only of a pair of pantaloons made of two pieces, a front and a seat, similarly cut, which were sewed together along the edges.

Tuesday, after the usual military drill, the crew was treated to a sharpshooting contest as a relief from monot-

ony. A target placed in a boat was towed about two
hundred yards astern, the men assembled on the stern deck
blazing away at it and making on the whole good hits. As
the sea was rough and the target reeled about in every
conceivable manner, a hit meant something, so that congratulations were in order.

On Wednesday, as the sea had again calmed down
sufficiently for coaling, the *Pontos* came upon our port,
and we took on fuel until Friday, the second of October.

The monotony of routine, of which the above gives some
idea, continued more than two or three days before new
excitement arose. At about twelve o'clock on the first night
of our coaling a hand shook me from my sleep, and I
started up to find Hoffmann bending over me.

"Wake up, old man!" he shouted. "Wake up and hear
the good news."

I raised myself, bewildered.

"Is the war over?" I asked.

"Not by a d—— sight," he retorted. "The *Emden*——"

"What, is the *Emden* alongside?"

"Not that, either. The *Emden* has captured six English
merchantmen in the Bay of Bengal, sunk five of them,
and sent their crews to Calcutta in the sixth. The news
just came. Think of it, Niezy! In the Bay of Bengal! Right
in the lion's mouth! Pulling his teeth! *Hein?* Worth waking
up to hear, *Hein?*"

I swore mentally at being waked out of a good sleep
even to hear the best news in the world but, as my watch

would soon begin and I should have had to get up anyway, I forgave Heinz and asked him to tell me a love story while I dressed.

Hoffmann, if I have not mentioned it, was a veteran lover. Being the best soul in the world, a good man from the bottom of his heart, trustworthy and of exemplary nicety in all his dealings, he yet never had luck in love. It seems that girls are afraid of "pattern men"; at least this was Hoffmann's experience.

When on shore he was forever falling madly in love, proposing, and, alas! being disastrously rejected. He said he always knew in advance that this would be the case, but some devil urged him on and he ran the course. As I was his closest friend on board and enjoyed his most secret confidences, he would spend hours in lonely lovelornness, telling me the course of the various unlucky episodes, which, he said, always ended by his putting his revolver to his temple and then taking it away again in the hope that perhaps his luck would turn.

This night, either because he was so full of the news of the *Emden,* or as I supposed because I so abruptly asked for one of his love stories, he became silent and I found myself doing the talking. Then when I suddenly looked up I found him staring at the ceiling, big tears rolling down his cheeks.

"For heaven's sake, Heinz," I cried, springing up. "What's the matter?"

"Nothing," he answered, looking away. Then he began

to laugh. "Don't mind me, Niezy, old man, I'm a d——
ass, that's all!"

And with this he told me that the picture of my mother
which I always kept hanging over the door of my cabin
had just reminded him that yesterday was his mother's
birthday and that in the excitement of work and watch he
had forgotten all about it.

"Then a bottle on it now," I said. "I have one in my
trunk." Whereupon I pulled out a bottle of champagne, a
present from my uncle, and the last of three bottles which
I had brought all the way from Europe. I was keeping it
for some tremendous occasion. But as I myself was just
going on duty, while Hoffmann on the contrary was on
the point of turning in I merely tasted the wine and left
my disconsolate friend the rest, which he proceeded to
enjoy like an epicure.

"To our mothers!" he toasted, "and may they be well
and happy and may they live to see us again."

It came from his heart. I prayed it might be so, but as
events fell it proved otherwise. Neither of us ever saw
his mother again. As I mentioned some time back, my
mother died before I reached home, and Hoffmann, poor
fellow, lost his life on the *Eclipse* while trying to get to
Germany. On me fell the duty of breaking the news to
his mother and family.

Chapter VIII

THE CAPTURE OF THE "LA CORREN-TINA" RAISES THE PRICE OF MEAT

ON FRIDAY, the second of October, we finished coaling from the *Pontos*. Then, our band playing "Es braust ein Ruf wie Donnerhall" and "Muss ich denn, muss ich denn, zum Städtchen hinaus," reinforced by a threefold hurrah! from both our crews, we steamed rapidly away. Once more alone on the bosom of the ocean, we settled down to cleaning ship.

A thorough renovation the vessel certainly needed. The decks were grimy, the staterooms dusty; everything white was spotted. Everywhere the all-soiling coal dust had found its way. A general scouring accordingly began. Scrubbing squads armed with long-handled brushes marched along deck like old-time street sweepers. There followed a rear guard wielding a hose which washed overboard the soapy scrubbings. Below decks mops and brooms were being plied, while aloft the brush was busy repainting the masts and upper decks.

Then, to cheer up the men after their strenuous course of duty, Commander Thierfelder announced that at four o'clock in the afternoon boat races would be held. This was welcome news. At 3:30 P. M. the engines stopped and all work on board ceased. The men hastily brushed up their uniforms, came on deck, and under my direction—I was sport officer of the ship—lowered six of our lifeboats into the water. These, manned with previously chosen crews, were soon rowed out to the starting point two hundred yards to starboard. The ship's launch at the same time put out with a crew of officers to superintend the starting of the races.

To distinguish the various entries, each boat carried a piece of coloured bunting lashed to its prow, while the various coaches who sat in the stern of their boats all wore in balbric fashion a band of bunting in colour identical with that at the prow of their boats. These colours lent a romantic touch to the event.

At 4 P. M. the first race started. I had designated as judges Lieutenant Fix and two other friends. These took their stations at our bow, where the finish was to be made, and where they could clearly see the progress of the race. In the distance, some two city blocks from the ship, the six small boats and the launch lay abreast each other, riding silently upon the gentle swells, their oars dipping at rest in the sea.

To start the race Lieutenant Fix raised his pistol and fired. At sight of the flash the six lifeless specks upon the ocean began to splash and move forward, slowly at first, then rapidly, sending up white splashes of spray from their bows as they nosed up and down over the gently rising water. Toward the prow of the *Kronprinz Wilhelm* they came sweeping, their crews bending in unison to the cry of the coaches.

Everyone knows what a boat race is like. At the same time that the boats sped forward out on the water, upon the decks of the *Kronprinz Wilhelm* four hundred husky throats shouted and cheered across the expanse of ocean, while on our forepeak the judge awaited the finish.

Of the six boats three soon took the lead; two of these in turn began to outdistance the third. All attention then was withdrawn from the remaining crews which, recognizing that the race was over for them, lay back on their oars to watch the white and red, who pulled as if their lives depended on the outcome.

From where I stood on the forepeak I could see that the race would be close, neither boat seeming in the lead. The crews were exceptionally well matched. Finally, within fifty feet of our prow, both coaches rose from their seats and shouted in quickened tempo. The faces of the men were strained, their teeth clenched,

At the tip of our ship Lieutenant Fix and his co-judges had mounted upon chairs, Fix holding a handkerchief over the boat's side. As the two boats swept past our prow to the starboard side the handkerchief dropped. One boat was a yard in advance of the other; the red coach had won.

The cheer that went up from the four hundred throats drowned for a few minutes all sense and sound. The boats turned about and their fagged crews clambered up our sides to be embraced and held up by our men. Some of the tired oarsmen stretched themselves out on deck exhausted, to get up again in a few minutes and stumble around, leaning on their mates.

A second race with fresh crews was soon begun. This proved as exciting as the first until near the end where one boat began to outdistance its competitors. As soon as this happened, the suspense was broken and the excitement dropped. Three more races were held that afternoon, all more or less exciting, but then the men had had enough.

Meanwhile, our lookouts had been especially watchful. The mood of our men was necessarily complex. While interest was centred upon the struggling oarsmen, in the background of consciousness the serious nature of our position as a ship of war in a time of war did not sleep. On the one hand we had to be alert lest in the midst of our sport an enemy warship surprise us; on the other it was the aim of the *Kronprinz Wilhelm* to see that no prize slip by in the excitement of the sport. At six o'clock the races were over and the men all back at their stations.

The days that followed were pleasant ones. Sunday was a day of rest for all hands, with a band concert in the afternoon, after which those men who had come to us from the *Pontos* were sworn into our service. On Tuesday the whole crew was again divided, this time into five divisions, the fifth division being placed under my command. As this happened to be the largest division, consisting of a hundred and twenty-five men, I had cause to be both proud of the honour and disgruntled at the work the command would entail. But the organization of our crew after we had taken a number aboard from the *Ebernburg,* the *Pontos,* and the *Prussia,* and lost others to those ships was at last complete.

Hardly had the ship achieved this smooth-working plan of personnel and put herself in a state of readiness for any event, when the long-awaited sight of a prize rewarded her. Wednesday the seventh of October, at six in the morning, the lookout spied a funnel to port. Over the edge of the morning sea a ship was rising into day.

All signs pointed to a swift-footed prize, so Commander Thierfelder decided upon a special mode of approach. He knew that if he allowed the *Kronprinz* to be recognized too soon he might have to give an extended chase, during which the enemy would use her wireless and call for help. He, therefore, used strategy in order to get near enough for prudent attack.

Turning the *Kronprinz* directly toward the stranger, which was heading our way, he slowed down the engines, keeping the *Kronprinz* almost stationary, but always with prow pointed toward the enemy. In this position the prize, now rapidly coming up, was unable to count our funnels or masts or to make out other marks of identification. We, on the other hand, had had a clear view of the approaching ship until it sighted us and headed our way. Through our glasses we soon made her out to be the *La Correntina.*

It was not until she came nearer, however, that the

splendid proportions of our prize were apparent. Then we beheld one of the prides of the sea. She was armed, too, with guns larger than our own.

"Now," I thought, "we are in for it."

"Clear for action!" had already been given and all men were at their stations. When the word came down that the enemy was armed the faces of our men lit up. They expected action and were ready for a fight.

The *La Correntina* made no motions of defence, evidently thinking us a British ship in distress, little dreaming that a German raider of our importance could be in these waters. When we were near enough she began signalling with a semaphore which was installed on her bridge. In reply Commander Thierfelder put on full speed, and the *Kronprinz Wilhelm,* already within range, swooped down upon the unsuspecting prize.

It was well for us we did so. Taken completely by surprise the *La Correntina* had no time to turn about to get away. She had either to surrender or fight. We expected her to give battle, but her captain being without ammunition for his guns had nothing to do but surrender.

A scene of excitement meanwhile took place on the decks of the surrendered ship. Men and women were to be seen rushing over the decks, some putting on life belts, others apparently trying to get the lifeboats ready for launching. Crew as well as passengers seemed panic-stricken, evidently thinking that the *Kronprinz Wilhelm* was going to sink the ship on the spot.

These fears were not allayed until our prize crew got into its boat and rowed over to the captured vessel. Our commander always selected large, hearty-looking men for prize-crew service so as to make a good impression on the enemy. In consequence the prize crew consisted largely of the ship's butchers. These, having round faces and fleshy sides, gave the enemy the impression that the German crews were composed of supermen, and that they were above all not in distress for lack of food.

The prize crew brought back word that the *La Correntina* was an English cold-storage steamer of Liverpool, returning from Buenos Aires on her maiden voyage—a twin screw, capable of seventeen to eighteen knots. We thus saw the wisdom of Commander Thierfelder's strategy. Had he not used the ruse of letting the enemy come up before attacking her she might have given him a two hours' chase and, in addition to making us burn our slender store of fuel, have brought us into the neighbourhood of enemy warships.

The ship proved a veritable mine. The vessel itself, newly built, was the last word in structure and equipment, her furnishings including a reserve rudder at her stern and a Mauser's light signalling apparatus on her bridge. She carried in all twelve good-sized lifeboats—provisions for a large number of passengers. Curiously, she bore triple derricks forward which, supplemented by her two masts and her smokestack, gave her a comblike appearance when viewed from the side. Except for her white cabin, lifeboats, and a thin strip running the length of her hull, she was entirely black, while at her stern there floated conspicuously a large British flag.

In the hold of this valuable prize rested seven and one half million pounds of frozen meat, one thousand eight hundred tons of bunker coal, and a plentiful supply of mixed provisions. Her two 117 mm. guns—of larger calibre and longer range than our own—proved no mean portion of the booty. In addition, we later found in the ship's hold twelve modern rifles and ammunition intended for the use of sharpshooters in defence of the ship. These guns became weapons of our ship's guard.

We now ordered the *La Correntina's* crew and twenty-six passengers—among the latter a number of reservists on their way to the theatre of war, all together about one hundred men—aboard our ship, according the neutral passengers the same freedom of the first-class quarters we had given those of the *Indian Prince*. The officers, crew, and reservists after being searched were given quarters in the second-class staterooms, where a guard was placed.

As before in the case of the *Indian Prince,* so now with the *La Correntina,* searching the captive passengers and crews as they came over our side afforded considerable amusement as well as much that was of interest. It seems that the first instinct of man in an emergency is to save what at that instant appears most precious to him. Little traits of character thus come to light. On the persons of some of our prisoners were found secreted letters, papers, pictures of loved ones, amulets, breviaries, and Bibles. Others bore weapons of various kinds, such as revolvers and stilettos. On several we discovered whisky, cards, and dice. Nearly every prisoner had something tucked away which with either innocent or sinister intent he had hoped to save from the general wreck. About the most popular articles of all, however, were knives, forks, spoons, and other such pieces of silverware as could be snatched in the last instant from galley or cabin. The crews were the offienders in this respect. They knew where such valuables were kept and invariably pilfered whatever they could find, no doubt with a patriotic view to saving it from going to the bottom. We took these articles from them, assuring them that all legitimate possessions would be given back later on.

Most of the prisoners quietly submitted to search as a matter of course. Some, however, strenuously objected. In such cases the search was not immediately forced. The officers in charge of the searching first reasoned with a man, explaining that he would later on get back all that was rightfully his. If he still objected he was felt all over to determine whether he had any weapons hidden in his clothing; then he was taken to a cabin by himself and told that he would receive no food until he submitted to search. This invariably brought the recalcitrant to terms. If, however, a man had still persisted in his refusal, he would have been taken out of the room and forcibly searched. But the threat of solitary confinement was in every case sufficient.

With the women prisoners the matter was different. As there were no women on board the *Kronprinz Wilhelm,* a search of the persons of women prisoners could not be made. We merely contented ourselves with their assurance that they carried no weapons. Those who looked suspicious, and later there were a few, were segregated and watched.

Great care was exercised in this searching, as much to see that no weapon got by unnoticed as to be sure that a record was taken of each article so that it might be identified and returned at a future time. We wanted no one to complain afterward that the official German ship *Kronprinz Wilhelm* had stolen his belongings. The officers in charge rendered strict account of their taking, these accounts being subject to check. It speaks not a little for their ability that, during a voyage in which more than a thousand prisoners passed weeks on our decks, not a single complaint was lodged against the officers in charge of belongings.

At 6 P. M. we sent aboard the *La Correntina* our fourth Division to man the vessel and get things in condition for transfer to our decks. While some of these men began dismantling the two guns of the ship, others unbolted and took down such parts of the vessel's machinery and fixtures as would be of use to us in our voyage.

During the next few days this work went on rapidly. By day the steamer lay alongside, while we coaled from her bunkers and transferred her supplies. At night we stood away, letting the vessel follow us while we steamed to a different location as emergency directed.

On the second day, while the cabin of the *La Correntina* was being searched, one of our men came upon a secret British wireless code book. This valuable find was immediately turned over to Brinkmann who set himself to master the code. He told me it cleared up many things that had been puzzling him for some time.

By Friday the two guns of the *La Correntina* had been hoisted upon our poop and bolted into place, one on each side of the vessel. Had other things been equal this would have brought our offensive armament up to four guns, doubling our security. But alas! For the new weapons we had not a single round of ammunition. In their present condition they would be chiefly valuable as camouflage or scarecrows, so that the *Kronprinz Wilhelm* was forced to hope that some good fortune would bring her the needed shells. This stroke of luck never fell, and from first to last the guns remained mere dummies, useful only as camouflage and for exercising the crews.

In this capacity, however, they did excellent service. Splendid pieces of English make, instead of having a side-loading breech mechanism like guns of German manufacture, they were loaded by withdrawing the hinged breech mechanism from the rear after the American fashion. At first our men did not like this arrangement, but they rapidly got used to it, and in the end they became very proficient in handling the guns.

The weather during the last days had been growing increasingly worse, the wind rising until the seas made coaling impossible. It was not until Wednesday of the next week that we finally finished taking over all the *La Correntina's* coal, provisions, and machinery. Then the task of sinking the ship began.

The work was practically the same as in the case of the *Indian Prince*. The bolts of the enormous cocks of the *La Correntina* had previously been greased and impedimenta removed. The seacock squad now climbed over to the vessel's decks, unbolted the seacocks, and clambered back to our side. Then the *Kronprinz* backed away some eight hundred to one thousand yards, taking great care to keep her prow pointing toward the settling ship so that none of the prisoners of war, all of whom were quartered aft on our vessel, might witness the sinking.

The *La Correntina,* however, sank too slowly for us. At 6 P. M., when Commander Thierfelder could wait no longer, he sent over a boat, had dynamite placed aboard the steamer and the fuse set. The explosion which followed seemed only partially successful. For although the ship sank rapidly at first, she soon rested at the same level. Suddenly, however, she started to sink again. At eight o'clock we began to hear a rumbling in her hold which soon increased to a dull thunder. Then with a tremendous crash the ship's boilers blew up, sending into the quiet night a lemon flare mingled with a cataract of steam and water. A moment later the ship disappeared under the sea.

As mentioned, the *La Correntina* had carried as her principal cargo seven and one half million pounds of frozen meat. We learned later on that when the news of her sinking reached London the price of meat went up two pence a pound over all England.

The *La Correntina* was sent to the bottom Wednesday night, the fourteenth of October. Until the following Friday we did not sight another ship, our crew being kept busy cleaning the newly begrimed vessel. Our port side, as usual after coaling, had again become a sorry spectacle of grime, dents, and scratches. Plates had to be caulked at once to stop the leaks, and the outer walls had to be repainted to make the side look respectable once more.

On Friday at 5:45 P. M., when this work was about completed, we sighted a single smokestack to the south. Unlike the *La Correntina* this vessel was not heading directly toward us but was passing along the edge of the horizon, so that we could not wait for her to come up but were forced to give chase.

The gong and bugle sounded "Clear for action!" All men came to station and everything was ready for attack, but the stranger, penetrating our purpose, changed her course and steamed away at full speed, so that, though we would soon have overtaken her because of our greater speed, darkness just then set in to her rescue.

To follow a vessel in the dark at such a distance was next to impossible, so no sooner did we lose sight of our intended prize than we gave her up as lost, and turning about in our former course steamed rapidly from the position.

The following Sunday, October eighteenth, and Monday were calendar days for the *Kronprinz Wilhelm,* the former being a complete day of rest for all on board. At noon the crew was assembled on the after deck and addressed by the commander who spoke of the significance of the great battle of October 18, 1813, and the added significance of the eighteenth of October in the years 1831 and 1861. Commander Thierfelder was to say the least a well-read man, his address as usual furnishing the men with food for meditation. I always noticed that after such an address the bearing of the men became more dignified.

Monday was important because it brought to our side the freight and passenger liner *Sierra Córdoba* of Bremen, of the North German Lloyd, which carried a welcome cargo of provisions, tobacco, cigarettes, beer, clothes, and coal. We could not begin coaling from her at once, however, as the wind had risen and was whistling over the sea, tossing us about heavily. Not until Thursday, the twenty-second, could provisioning begin, when the sea being calmer we made the *Sierra Córdoba* fast at our port.

This day happened to be the birthday of the German Empress. In ordinary times we would have set the afternoon aside as a holiday. But now, under the pressure of utmost necessity, there was not a minute to lose from work, as the sea might begin rising again at any hour to put a stop to our coaling. This evening, however, in honour of the Empress, each man received half a litre of beer to celebrate the anniversary.

By nightfall, Friday, we had taken from the hold of the *Sierra Córdoba* one thousand tons of coal, together with extensive quantities of provisions and clothes. Our prisoners of war from the *La Correntina* were now transferred to the decks of the *Sierra Córdoba,* where some of our ship's guard were stationed over them. Then we steamed away, intending to meet the *Sierra Córdoba* again in a few days.

The Sunday following once more brought good cheer to the crew. The weather was clear but not too hot, with a light sea running, and the men stretched out on deck with the feeling that the world was not so bad after all. Early in the morning Commander Thierfelder ordered that each man be given a litre of beer, explaining that this was the reward for the labour of unloading the cargo of the *Sierra Córdoba,* much of which consisted of beer. Then in the afternoon when the band had treated us to a concert, athletic contests were announced.

Now in front of the forward bridge of our ship midway between port and starboard there stood a permanent horizontal bar on which acrobatic feats could be performed. It is a matter of pride to every German to be able to do feats of agility and strength upon such apparatus, so that from simple kips and knee turnovers to handstands and giant swings, all manner of acrobatic feats were performed this day in the open air under a cloudless sky, as our huge ship slowly rose and fell on a gentle sea. The men did their hardest *Turnen* or acrobatics in the most polished form, knowing that they were being as rigidly judged by their hypercritical fellows as if they were under the eyes of the masters in the training halls at home.

After the acrobatics followed a strenuous tug-of-war on the promenade deck between two teams of fifty men each. Barefooted and bareheaded, their sleeves rolled up above the elbow, they grasped a three-inch hempen cable. At the fall of the commander's hand they began tugging for life, a ship's hose meanwhile playing upon the empty stretch of rope between the two teams, so that the losing side would be forced to pass through a deluge. Tugging, straining, clenching their teeth, both sides bent their muscles to the trial. Soon the stern-enders began dragging the bow-men over the mark, but just as the latter were about to pass into the spout of water the flow suddenly ceased. Someone had turned the water off below decks. Instantly the howl went up from the winning stern-enders. In high dudgeon they dropped the rope and set off like a band of Indians, whooping and swearing, in search of the culprit. The guilty man, however, was never found, and when everything had quieted down again it was too late in the afternoon to repeat the contest. There were other games to be played, and the programme must be carried out, no matter who should lose by it. So the stern-enders were mollified by being formally awarded the victory. Hurdle races and sack races followed with their usual accompaniments of cheers and shouting. At last, tired but exhilarated, the men were ordered to get ready for the evening meal.

After supper when the whole crew was assembled on the after deck, prizes were distributed to the winners of the contests, all of whom good-naturedly shared them with the losers. Cigars, cigarettes, and wine thus passed around, and the jolly seamen settled down to games of cards, dominoes, checkers, and chess, supplemented by "craps" or dice in private corners, until the evening at last closed as enthusiastically as the morning had begun.

But if Sunday had been a day of revelry, Monday was a day of no less excitement. For Commander Thierfelder thought that an opportune time had now come to give the crew a trial at lifesize target practice. This should exercise not only our two forward guns, but the machine gun and the small arms of the ship's guard as well.

For a time the crew was given a floating target nine hundred metres distant at which the sharpshooters popped away merrily doing what execution they could. Then an old boat was rigged up and set adrift. At a distance of six thousand metres the *Kronprinz Wilhelm* turned about and steered full speed upon it. When we came within three thousand metres of the little craft the big guns let fly firing twelve shots apiece. Then at nine hundred metres our machine gunners and sharpshooters opened fire. It would have been dangerous to be in that boat. Most of the shots told, so that when we came up with the remains of the little craft not much was left of it. The wreckage we carefully gathered up to prevent giving the enemy a clue as to our presence. The men that day laid down their weapons with a feeling that come what might the *Kronprinz Wilhelm* would give a good account of herself in actual action with the enemy.

A few days later as I was passing up the port stairway to the bridge at four in the morning to go on watch, I met an orderly on his way down. He was holding a handkerchief to his nose.

"Nose bleeding?" I asked.

"Yes," he grumbled. "I blew the bottom out of it just now. Going down to my bunk and lie on my back. That always stops it. But this means that we're going to capture another ship soon."

I looked at him again to see whether he was joking but he seemed serious.

"How's that?" I questioned.

He answered with all sincerity,

"Every time my nose has bled thus far we've captured a ship within twenty-four hours. My nose bled the night before we captured the *Indian Prince* and again on the evening before we got the *La Correntina*. Now it's bleeding harder than ever, so I suppose we'll get a big one this time."

I chuckled as I went up on the bridge.

"Curious notions," I thought. "And now if we should capture a ship to-morrow that fellow will consider his superstition as proved."

Chapter IX

A WOMAN CREATES FRICTION : WE COAL FROM THE "UNION" UNDER DIFFICULTIES

AT 4 A. M. my watch began. It was the morning of the twenty-eighth of October and our ship was cruising only forty miles from the coast of Uruguay. To add to our danger we were in a sea where the neighbourhood was policed by enemy craft.

From the bridge I looked into the beautiful night. In the rotunda of the skies the large stars twinkled brightly— reflected in the uneven sea below. Over the distant horizon the Southern Cross stood out like a sacred emblem, while near by the incomparable image of Orion strode over the heavens, the three diamonds in his belt flashing down like signal lights. Just over the top of our forward mast lay the brilliant Canopus of the ship Argo, while to its left crouched the two giant centaurs which so steadfastly guard the Southern Cross. It was one of the most splendid displays of heavenly grandeur I had ever seen.

Far above me at the masthead I could see the men in the lookout bending their search toward the circle of the horizon, while still higher up against the very stars perched the little crow's nest with its single occupant. I thought of my first day in the crow's nest some fifteen years before. That was no pleasant experience.

The crow's nest of a ship is no comfortable place for a new man. As the mast rocks violently with each toss of the ship, seasickness soon overcomes him. There is no sensation like it—not even that felt on first riding on a camel's hump. Then there is the feeling of uncertainty, of lack of adequate support. Peering down from the dizzy height the ship below looks as thin and frail as a match stem. To fall means death. In a storm one holds on by the teeth.

Once in a storm I saw a sailor lose his hold. As he fell his body struck one of the booms of the derricks. I heard a dull thud, then a shriek or rather a sound like the death squeal of a pig, and the man went over into the sea. He was never found.

I thought of the foggy days when the man in the crow's nest sits high over the blanket of fog; when he can see nothing of his own ship or of the hulls of other ships but beholds the tops of the masts of strange vessels and can almost hail the lookouts who like him are perched over the roof of the fog. Then the great hot sun comes slowly up and it is day for him while all is still dusk on deck in fog below.

And when the fog clears and distant ships come over the horizon the man in the crow's nest is struck with the patent rotundity of the earth. He no longer wonders at the guesses of Columbus. How is it possible to see the ships rise from behind the spherical sea—first the topmasts, then the sails, bit by bit lower, finally the cabin and hull—without perceiving that the earth is a ball?

All these thoughts ran through my mind that early morning as I looked out over the South Atlantic waters. By degrees the twinkling stars began to grow more dim. The bowl of heaven took on a deep and deeper blue, then in the east a few streaks of purple turned to gold and the sun slowly peeped up over a silver ocean. Soon the ship would awake to another hot day.

Suddenly on the stillness of the morning the voice from the crow's nest rang out:

"Ship, eight points to port."

I turned my glasses in the direction indicated. There was nothing to be seen. A minute of quiet, then the lookout rang its bell. It too had sighted the ship. I accordingly rang the gong. The bugle sounded, the drummer rolled his drum, and the signal "Clear for action!" raised the sleeping ship.

In a few moments the men came rushing on deck, passing swiftly to their stations. No moment was lost, for they were thoroughly trained. Three minutes after the gong had sounded the ship was ready for attack or defence.

I could now see with the aid of my glasses that there was no need of haste, for the ship sighted was a sailing vessel which we could soon overtake at an easy gait. Commander Thierfelder, who had now taken command of the bridge, took the situation in at a glance, gave the *Kronprinz* a leisurely speed to save coal and steered in the direction of the sail.

At 8 A. M., after a cruise of two and one half hours, we came within hailing distance of a four-masted bark whose name and nationality we obtained by the use of the international flagging code. It was the French bark *Union* of Bordeaux on her way from Cardiff, which port she had left on the fifth of September for Montevideo. The ship which had already been on her way fifty-one days bore a cargo of three thousand one hundred tons of Cardiff coal— a most welcome article—provisions, tobacco, and wine.

The crew of the *Union*, consisting of a captain, three officers, and twenty-six men, were commanded to bundle up their belongings and come over to our decks, being warned at the same time that everything left would be regarded as war booty. They accordingly came over to us loaded like pack mules, not excepting the officers.

It is hard to conceive of how much a man can carry if he has to. The load which the first officer of the *Union* brought, partly carrying and partly slung all about him, consisted of a foot-locker, full and heavy, two telescope satchels also loaded to bursting, about three suits, two blankets, an overcoat, some navigation instruments wrapped in a piece of tarpaulin, and other odds and ends. The man was almost hidden from view. He got stuck on the ladder and was ready to fall back on deck when one of our crew climbed down and helped him up.

Lieutenant Ruedebusch, who stood beside me watching the performance, facetiously remarked that we would do well to give the same order to every crew we captured, as it would save us time in unloading.

As we were at this time only forty miles off the coast of Uruguay, longitude 50 degrees west, latitude 35 degrees south, in an important ocean lane, it behooved us to take our prize in tow at once and steer farther out to sea. We accordingly made all haste to begin the work.

A corps of former sailors was dispatched aboard the *Union* to put everything in readiness; the prize was then taken in tow, and we steamed off to east by north as fast as we could safely drag her.

A race now began between time, our coal hoard, and the weather. As the *Kronprinz* was short of coal, while in the hold of the captured bark were three thousand one hundred tons, Commander Thierfelder was only too anxious to bring the *Union* alongside and begin coaling. The sea, however, had risen to such a pitch that coaling could not be thought of, and we were forced to wait for a settling of the weather.

Meanwhile, our own crew aboard the bark —all men with previous experience on sailing vessels—had begun to take down sails and rigging, lashing everything into bundles ready for transference to our decks when the sea should become calm. These men suffered such hardships that I shall soon let one of them, my personal friend, Frank Fehlkamm, tell of his experiences on the bark.

While we were thus steaming along to the northeast on Sunday, the first of November, we were again joined by the *Sierra Córdoba,* which according to agreement had returned with our guard and their prisoners. The *Sierra Córdoba* had nothing in particular to report, was glad to see us with a captured vessel, and at once took her position steaming in our wake, while from time to time our band played over to her from our stern to brighten the hours of her crew and her prisoners of war.

By this time our fuel was so low that if an enemy warship had surprised us we would not have had much chance of getting away. Conscious of our danger, we repeatedly attempted to bring the *Union* on our port to begin coaling, but each time the tossing seas sweeping the low decks of the bark would have swamped her had we continued our attempts. In the end we were forced to abandon all hope of coaling from her in a heavy sea. In fact, in the course of these attempts the wooden scuppers of the *Union* were badly damaged, the lives of the brave crew aboard her being imperilled again and again. How they got through that "voyage of horrors," as they afterward spoke of it, without losing some men is hard to understand.

An episode aboard the *Union* now occurred which for its picturesque touch of romantic irony will keep the *Union* ever fresh in my memory.

It so happened that the *Union,* a bark of the old-fashioned type, bore below her bowsprit a wooden figurehead in the form of a beautiful woman. The figure was neatly carved and painted and was truly a work of art. Our chief doctor, being a man of taste, got Commander Thierfelder's permission to take it down as his personal prize, but as it was too late to begin work on the image that day the matter was postponed until next morning.

That night many of us were jealous of the doctor. Now that the figure was his property each of us wished he had asked for it first, for it would make a splendid trophy for our halls at home. It occurred to me that perhaps the lucky officer would sell the figure and I was beginning to have hopes of ultimately buying the maiden.

What was our consternation, therefore, when next morning on looking at the *Union* we beheld only the torso of the beautiful figure; the head had been struck from its shoulders and lost. The doctor went into a tantrum. He swore that some personal enemy had committed the vandalism to spite him. We made a search for the head but without success. If report can be trusted the doctor was so disappointed he went to his cabin and cried, and to be frank I felt pretty bad myself. The maid was fair, and even a wooden woman if beautiful is a joy to look upon when one is marooned with one's own sex upon the high seas in a ship that cannot come to land.

While we were thus steaming slowly onward waiting for the sea to become calm, the heavens by good fortune let down a drenching rain, as welcome to us as it had been to our old friend the Ancient Mariner who had once cruised in exactly these parts, though under somewhat different circumstances. But instead of resting content with blessing the rain, we made efforts to catch it in sheets

The Sierra Córdoba *and the French* Union.

The Union *acknowledges defeat after a dramatic battle with high seas.*

of canvas which we spread out on deck, diverting the water into our tanks by means of hose, for by this time the *Kronprinz* was badly in need of fresh water.

With the rain that night of the fourth of November came news from Germany which put new spirit into the jaded crew. The two large German cruisers, *Scharnhorst* and *Gneisenau,* had met four English cruisers of equal size and had sunk two and cut up the other two badly before they had saved themselves from further destruction by flight. Of all enemies the crew especially disliked the British, so that now the men gave three thunderous cheers for the *Scharnhorst* and the *Gneisenau*. These night howls bursting upon the quiet hum of the ship excited our prisoners who, ignorant of the cause, began to suspect a mutiny afoot. At last, however, peace reigned again and the men turned in to get some sleep which they knew might be broken at any minute by the gong sounding "Clear for action!"

As stated, the sea was yet too rough to permit us to bring the *Union* alongside. Our need of coal, however, was urgent. We must get it at any cost. Commander Thierfelder, being a man of resources, now rose to the occasion. If the *Union* could not be coaled from, the *Sierra Córdoba,* a much larger vessel, could. There was nothing to do but rob our sister ship. On Friday the sixth we accordingly ordered the *Sierra Córdoba* on our port and began taking on coal and provisions as fast as the pitching of our vessel permitted. Meanwhile, we also used the favourable opportunity to transfer to the *Sierra Córdoba* the captured crew of the *Union*. The officers we still retained in our cabins, for, like their predecessors of the *Indian Prince,* they refused to sign the necessary promise not to make war on Germany during the present struggle.

At six-thirty the *Sierra Córdoba* let go our side for the night to return again next day, when eight men from her crew came over to take service on our ship. These men, who were all well picked for our needs, congratulated themselves upon being able to serve on board the history-making *Kronprinz Wilhelm,* and as new men are always welcome aboard ship, especially to a crew that has so long been away from all other human beings, our men were glad to have them.

The sea now became appreciably calmer. The commander seizing the opportunity let go the steamer, brought the *Union* alongside, and took on coal and provisions, rushing the work with all possible speed, since at any moment the wind might rise again and bring the operation to a halt. Commander Thierfelder stood constantly by the men, encouraging them by word as well as by presence.

"Now, men," he would say, "keep the line going. The sea is rising. The life of the ship depends on it. That's the way!"

The men thus worked like demons, but as was expected the sea soon became rough again, so that we could no longer risk taking the little bark on our port. But as it was a matter of life and death to continue taking on coal, Commander Thierfelder tried the expedient of coaling from our poop by means of a cable and running tackle stretched over to the bark. This process was slow and in the end unsatisfactory.

On Sunday at 4 P. M. all hands were given a holiday. Then at five our commander assembled the crew and addressed them concerning their achievements. The *Kronprinz Wilhelm* had now been on the ocean out of sight of land and in a state of constant vigilance for one quarter of a year. During this time she had cruised 15,155 miles— over one half the distance around the earth—and had captured two British steamships and a French bark, a total of 13,558 gross tons. In addition, large quantities of valuable stores had been either confiscated or sunk. The commander congratulated the crew on its courageous energy and continued good cheer. The German Fatherland had reason to be proud.

While the ship, further, was in excellent condition and ready for conquest, the wireless had brought news that the Allied press had three times already proclaimed the *Kronprinz* no longer afloat. In August, 1914, the newspapers had said she had been towed into Bermuda; in September they affirmed that she had been sunk by an English torpedo boat off Fernando de Noronha; in October the Brazilian papers had announced that she had been sunk by the armed merchantman *La Correntina.* If, he concluded, the Allied press should continue to destroy the ship at this rate there was good hope that the *Kronprinz* might be of much further service to the Fatherland.

This patriotic speech seemed to bring better weather, for next day it was possible to have the *Union* alongside, when for the first time coaling from her was done to advantage. We also used the evener decks to take aboard ample quantities of wine contained in great casks in her hold; the men were naturally much interested in this part of the consignment. Two live and squealing pigs were also hoisted over to us; a third had unfortunately been killed when a falling spar of the *Union* broke its back.

These two animals at once became objects of amusement. It so happened that at just this time some of our men had been detailed to paint a portion of the upper deck the usual sea-gray. As the pigs came aboard a bright idea struck one of the painters, and with the help of some comrades who held the animals for him he painted fantastic designs all over their bodies. Then another sailor got some green paint from the storeroom and painted eyes, noses, and mouths on the creatures in conspicuous places. The pigs were now chased down the promenade deck to the intense delight of everybody.

There still remained on board the *Union* a large flock of chickens which we were to take aboard at the earliest opportunity. These fowl presented a most comical spectacle on deck in mid-ocean. They strutted about with greatest unconcern, swooping down upon flies or chasing them to the edge of the deck, warily eyeing us when we made an unexpected motion, giving warning calls to each other if they saw a man climb aloft the rigging; acting, in short, as if they were being interrupted in their own barnyard or village street by the coming up of some band of sightseers. Their cackling, cawing, and "Kikeriki!" made many of us homesick. At nightfall they took refuge in their chicken house—a veritable castle.

Aboard sailing craft it is a custom, handed down from ancient times, to have a chicken house on board, of the most artistic design. As a Christmas present to the master, the ship's carpenter and the blacksmith spend weeks of their spare time constructing a gable-roofed house upon stilts in the aft part of the ship. Under the gables of the roof they fix artistic wooden figures, carved in the form of dragons, long-tailed, monsters, and upon the coping of the roof is usually perched a wooden cock. The whole is painted in a fitting variety of colours and this chicken palace is usually the most interesting fixture of the ship.

The chicken house of the *Union* was an especially elaborate one, resplendent with neat and quaint figures painted in gay colours. The chickens, which knew very well where to find it, made much ado before entering for the night. Every once in a while when all were inside, a sudden rumpus would arise, whereupon one of the fowls would unceremoniously come fluttering out, evidently knocked off the roost. The disgruntled bird would then sagely look about for a few minutes like some gallant scout sent out for the purpose, then strut back to the doorway, and with much excitement from within fly back to the roost.

Our men gave the chickens names, such as Betty, and Lisa, and Old Fritz, some humorously inquiring of our prisoners whether any of the fowl were pedigreed. Still others attached pieces of bread to strings and enjoyed the sport of jerking the bait away from the chickens that scrambled after it. The little comedy of these so-out-of-place chickens thus gave our men much enjoyment.

The two weeks that followed saw but a repetition of the daily routine of coaling. On some days the weather was calm, when we coaled with all speed; on others it became too rough for work, when the low-lying *Union* was swept again and again by the high-running wash and the lives of her heroic crew were imperilled. When coaling could not be done our crew was set to cleaning ship or put to battle practice—always something to keep the men busy, a cardinal necessity on a cruise like this.

It was now Friday, the twentieth of November, three weeks since the first taking of the *Union*. A stiff wind was blowing up, so that the bark was forced to stand off from our sides. When I looked from the stormy sky to the wind-swept sea and beheld the tossing bark rocking about without control of propeller or sail, I could not help saying to Lieutenant Fix: "Those men will see some fun to-night."

In fact, I should not have been surprised to find them gone to the bottom in the morning.

Fix shrugged his shoulders.

"We ought to take them off before it's too late," he said. "There are only eight hundred tons or so of coal left in the bark. . . . Eight hundred tons is a good bit," he added.

The wind increased, and the *Union* rocked like a log, her masts swaying from side to side through an angle of ninety degrees. I began to get worried. Night came on and still the wind increased. The *Kronprinz* herself was no longer a sober girl.

"Fix," I said after evening mess, "this is a serious business—this of the *Union*. I wonder why Thierfelder left the men aboard her."

"Eight hundred tons is a good deal of coal," was all he answered. But I could see that he also was worried. He knew what must be going on in that bark, for like every German naval officer he had seen service on such a ship. And a bark at the mercy of a storm is no comfortable habitation.

Saturday morning dawned on a storm-angry sea. I was up at daybreak to look for the *Union*. Hardly had I spied her, however, rolling and tossing like a splinter, when my attention was distracted by the voice of the lookout: "Sail, two points to starboard!"

Immediately "Clear for action!" sounded. On the foamy sea at the edge of the horizon three masts were pointing at the sky.

Chapter X

ADRIFT THREE WEEKS IN A BARK
ON HIGH SEAS

BEFORE speaking of the events which this latest ship brought, I should like to give you the narrative of my friend, Franz Fehlkamm, who spent three weeks of toil and privation on the ill-starred *Union*. What follows, though in my own words, is transcribed from notes which Franz Fehlkamm dictated.

"When word was brought me by a friend that I had been selected to go aboard the *Union* I was overjoyed, for the new labours would mean a change from the monotony aboard the *Kronprinz Wilhelm*. I had served my time as a seaman on just such a sailing vessel as the *Union,* and the old sailor's blood in my veins rose when I thought of climbing into the topmasts again and furling sails in the teeth of the wind at the base of the sky. Little did I dream what the *Union* had in store.

"There were two officers and fifteen men of us, all picked for our seaman's record. Once we were aboard the bark the command came down:

" 'First-class seamen, report !'

"I came up before the mast with some ten others and

received my first orders. As the *Union* and the *Kronprinz Wilhelm* were in dangerous waters, only forty miles from the coast of Uruguay, and we might be sighted by an Allied warship at any moment, it had been decided that the *Union* should not proceed under her own sail, which would take her too long, but must be towed. Our first work was therefore to haul in and fasten the towline of the mother ship, but as it would take some time to get the tackle ready we must meanwhile furl the *Union's* sails.

"The *Union's* sails! There was almost a square mile of canvas on that ship. The bark, which was square-rigged, had four tall masts carrying twenty-nine sails all told, some of them veritable circus tents. A crew of twenty-six men was needed to manage that ship and we were only fifteen.

"We began with the bottommost sails, the foresail, then the mainsail, and so on, furling the lowest one of each mast, after which we left the safe proximity of the deck and climbed into the rigging. I can see my comrades now, scrambling like squirrels along the ropes of the *Union*, working fast upon a pitching ship. To every yard we made the sails fast, lashing the *Zeissings* tightly around them. Everything went with rush and vigour, for the work was as yet an agreeable pleasure.

"When the time came for making clear the towing tackle—a more difficult task than furling the sails—we used as our towing anchor the so-called *Vorrunner* of the starboard anchor chain. The work of unwinding the chain and hoisting the anchor from the hawser hole to the deck was spared us, as the latter already lay neatly lashed upon the forecastle head, evidently merely stored until the ship should have run into harbour. We had only to drag the anchor chain from the bit by the use of the capstan and then to wait for the *Kronprinz Wilhelm*.

"The latter had by this time gotten the two-inch steel towline ready upon her starboard deck, the line being as long as the *Kronprinz Wilhelm* herself. The great ship then steamed up, shot us a line, and in a short time we had fastened down the steel tow. A six-ply tackle at the other end was fixed to a steel wire which ran around a roller on the poop of the *Kronprinz,* this arrangement being intended to take in the slack when it was necessary to bring the bark alongside. All now clear, we gave the signal, and the *Kronprinz Wilhelm* began to steam off slowly towing us after her.

"As it had by this time become dark and active work for that day was at an end, our commanding officer set up night watches in three shifts: 8–12, 12–4, 4–8. These were held every night through clear weather and through storm of the three weeks which were spent aboard the fated ship. In addition, we posted a lookout and placed a man at the wheel, for though we were in tow the rudder was still useful. This first night passed quietly, so that on the twenty-ninth of October we rose early with renewed energy to continue the work of making everything clear.

"After breakfast the command came down to cant the yards so that we might be brought alongside the *Kron-*

prinz Wilhelm. The yards of the *Union* were long heavy beams, projecting far out over the sides of the ship. We climbed aloft and began to work. When that was done, we were ordered to take down all sails—a difficult task as there was now a heavy sea running, and our ship being without sail and in tow was fairly at the mercy of the sea.

"In the midst of the stormy day a seaman named Joseph Zelinka and I were sent to the topmost yards to take down the sails, fold them into bundles, and let them safely down to deck. The wind piped and whistled, the masts swayed so that we several times almost lost our hold, but finally, after almost all-day's work for a week in the clouds, the work was finished, and we were back upon the rocking decks, congratulating ourselves on being alive.

"The sea, however, had become so rough and our ship so unmanageable without sails that we thought to better matters by rigging up some gaff sails for the easier control of the vessel. This work was soon done, but in the end was of little service to us, for though the ship rode slightly better than before she was nevertheless an unsteady thing to be upon.

"Our work was meanwhile not a little handicapped by the fact that we found all wires and bolts rusted fast, so that untackling was a matter of using hammer and cold chisel. This made the work slow, laborious, and often dangerous, as a man had to use both hands in the operation, clinging to the swaying and jerking rigging by his legs and arms as best he could. Yet this very difficulty was in a certain measure our saving, as it necessitated the sending over to us from the *Kronprinz Wilhelm* of forty additional men, who helped us during the day and left our ship each night.

"In the course of this work there was only one accident and that of a minor nature. This happened to my friend Zelinka, who mashed his finger when a loose chain fell from a yard upon the deck. It was this same seaman who later did such good and dangerous service in making fast the towline to the *Anne de Bretagne*.

"One thing of importance now happened which came near being our finish. On the sixth night of our stay on the *Union*, when everything in the rigging had been made ready for taking down, I was on watch from 12 to 4 A. M. At about two-thirty in the morning a spar at the top of our mainmast suddenly jolted loose, broke the chain that held it to its mast, and with a shower of sparks from its rattling chain plunged from its height into the sea on our port side. Had the ship's masts been vertical at the time, the spar would have struck our decks point-on and would have cut its way through the very bottom of the ship. It goes without saying that a hole in such an inaccessible part of the hold would have speedily sunk the vessel.

"When everything was ready for coming alongside the *Kronprinz*, Commander Thierfelder decided that he wanted three long spars of the *Union* taken down and hoisted upon the steamer to be used as fenders, in addition to a mast of the *Union*, which was to be planted upon the poop of the

Kronprinz for our Marconi wireless captured from the *Indian Prince*. This wireless station was already installed, lacking only its antenna. After much labour the *Union's* mast was unstemmed, hoisted to the decks of the *Kronprinz,* and planted, after which the antenna, ready on deck, was run up and the new station was ready for sending.

"The weather had by this time risen into a veritable storm, so that life aboard the *Union* was becoming unbearable. The bark was nothing more than a driving wreck upon mountainous seas, but as our hold was full of valuable stores, especially of coal, it was of utmost importance to keep the vessel afloat. The *Union,* furthermore, was leaking badly, so that the pumps had to be kept going night and day. As these were hand operated our crew settled down to continuous exercise to keep the hold clear. When one takes into consideration that this work went on upon a ship tossing twenty to thirty degrees upon both sides, the achievement will be seen to have been no mean one.

"Joseph Zelinka and I were still detailed to topmast duty —he with his mashed finger. I know that I often had all I could do to keep from being thrown overboard. How my comrade with his wounded hand got safely through the work is a mystery to me. But it seems that a man can get used to anything. I saw my friend hold a cold chisel in one hand and a machinist's hammer in the other and work doggedly on in the dizzy heights cutting rusty bolts and chains, while tears ran down both cheeks because of the pain in his open wound. The only time I remember his complaining was when he hit his hand with the hammer Then he gave vent to the choicest profanity I had heard in many a day.

"An old German proverb runs: 'There is good resting after completed work.' But for us this was not the case. There was only work, work, work, and no rest as long as we were aboard that bark. Each day brought a different task. When the weather lightened and we came alongside the *Kronprinz,* our toil did not lessen. If anything it increased. It must be remembered that we had no engines aboard to do our hoisting, all lifting being done by the use of pulleys and the capstan, round and round which we pushed and struggled many a thousand circuits. 'Muscle-steam' we called this work, which corresponds to the landsman's term 'Shanks's mare.' It is true there was donkey engine aboard the *Union,* but the contraption was so out of order that we could not make it run.

"To enliven matters, on the twelfth day, as our ship tossed about in the careering sea, the starboard anchor chain suddenly broke from its lashings. There was a deafening rumble, a cloud of rust dust flew into the air, and with an unearthly shriek the whole ponderous chain slid like a snake over our side into the blue sea. Not much damage was done, however; the *Union* had a second, the port anchor chain, which kept to its bits and did not glide into the sea until the twenty-second of November, when the bark itself went to the bottom.

"Meanwhile, coaling continued with all vigour, Commander Thierfelder coming to the rail of the *Kronprinz* to shout encouragement down to us. Yet the weather kept changing intermittently from better to worse, frequently putting a stop to the work of coaling. Unfortunately, the *Union* was an old bark. Built in 1878, she was now thirty-eight years of age, and her bottom had seen much repair. As a result of continual rubbing against the sides of the *Kronprinz* she soon began to leak so fast that pump as we would we could not keep her hold free. The water seeped in through a thousand seams, especially on the starboard side. As they dug out the coal our men soon came to a soggy bottom below which digging was impossible because the shovel only filled with black water.

"On the nineteenth of November there was still 933 tons of coal left in the bark's hold. The wind after a short abatement had once more risen into a gale and our vessel, no longer at the *Kronprinz Wilhelm's* side, tossed madly about. We now began to pray that Commander Thierfelder would give up trying to get the remaining coal and would call us back to the *Kronprinz*. This, however, he had no intention of doing. So long as there was the remotest possibility of getting out the rest of the coal he was determined to spare no pains to keep the bark afloat. He accordingly commanded the officers of our bark to keep us at the pumps.

"The *Union* was by this time a floating hell. We were gambling with death. We bent our backs at the pumps until our muscles gave out. Then we dropped down and rested and got up again to take our turn. Food came to us half-cooked and was eaten as we worked. For the water in the hold had to be pumped out. But our labour was lost. It was a Sisyphean labour. We pumped out a spoonful and a bucketful ran in.

"The ship was meanwhile beginning to list heavily to starboard. The coal in her hold, wet until it was only a blackened gruel, had shifted to that side, this shifting becoming greater with every lunge of the ship. In fact, the bark was listing some twenty degrees.

"On the night of the twentieth, as I stood watch between 8 and 12 P. M., Lieutenant Hoffmann detailed me from duty at the rudder to go forward with a seaman named Leers to look after the oil at the bow oil holes. Now, in times of storm it is policy on the ocean, especially on sailing vessels, to distribute oil over the waters at the ship's bow, so that the wind striking a slippery sea may glance off without lifting the water and causing it to leak over the vessel's side. To do this two holes in the ship's bows are used, one on each side of the vessel. A funnel-shaped container inside the ship which communicates by a vertical tube with the outside is plugged up with old waste or rags and a few gallons of oil are poured in. The oil seeps through the cotton plug and so out over the surface of the sea.

"As we two worked our way forward in the pitch dark night to replenish the oil in these containers I remembered the words of Lieutenant Hoffmann. Knowing the danger of the trip in such a sea, the good lieutenant had not directly ordered us out, though this would of course have been his right. He had merely said:

"'If you want to do all hands a great favour, you'll try to get to the oil ports and replenish the supply of oil. It will be for the best of everyone on board.'

"The night, I repeat, was pitch dark. At first we could not see our hands before our faces. Soon, however, our eyes became accustomed to the darkness and we began groping our way forward. The wind was blowing a gale, piping and howling and moaning like the day of doom. For two days we men had not had a dry stitch of clothing. Chattering with cold, Leers and I forged on ahead toward the bow.

"I was in the lead. As a guide I was using a long hand line which had been stretched from the stern to the forecastle head. As we proceeded it was continually necessary for us to pause until the ship took a moment's rest before plunging up or down another high sea. Then, in these moments of rest, we worked along as fast as possible until the next plunge began. After what seemed to us a half hour's struggle we reached the starboard oil house, entered, and replenished the supply of oil in the container which was empty. Then we came out on deck again to make our way to the port side for the same purpose.

"But at the moment that we came on deck a sudden tremor ran through the ship. The next instant we found ourselves clinging to whatever came handy, up to our shoulders in water. I thought the ship was sinking. Not giving up, however, Leers and I held on and waited. My hand still clung convulsively to the oil can.

"For a short time the water did not seem to subside. Then after what seemed an age it went down as fast as it had risen, and we were again able to slide over the deck.

"I tried to collect my wits. Something was radically wrong somewhere. But there was no more need of going to the port oil container. If the ship was going to plunge like this no oil could help her more. Besides, we had been only *asked* to do the task, not *ordered*, and in a case such as this we thought our lives worth more than an accomplished errand. So without more ado we began to make our way back to the cabin at the stern.

"Hardly had we reached the foremast, however, when the plunge of the ship repeated itself, and again I found myself up to my armpits in a boiling sea. When the plunge began I could not see Leers, but I heard his panting a foot behind me. As the water gripped me I heard my mate suddenly cry out; then I dashed into the shelter of the donkey-engine house.

"Leers, I thought, as the water rushed about my chin and I held on literally by my teeth, Leers has gone overboard.

"When the water subsided, I shouted at the top of my voice: 'Leers! Leers!'

"No answer. Then I remember swearing somewhat, after which, biting my teeth together, I gripped the line and started once more toward the stern. But hardly had I reached the mainmast when a third sea broke over the deck, sending another tremor through the ship. Seizing hold of a cleat on the mast, I held fast, sheltered by the size of the mast itself. But for this shelter I would have been torn loose and washed overboard. As it was, so strong was the plunge of the water that at first I gave myself up for lost.

"This sea soon subsided, however, and I was about to go on again, when suddenly my attention was attracted by a dark object swimming back and forth some twenty feet away. For an instant, as I peered through the dark with eyes accustomed to the night, I thought it was the body of my friend Leers. I was about to dash forward to take hold of it, when I recognized that it was too large for a man. With a rush the truth came over me. It was the remains of the aft hatchway tarpaulin cover, which had been torn loose. The hatch was uncovered.

"A hatch uncovered in a sea like this! It was suicide. A few more such rushes of water over the deck and the *Union* would fill and sink. I shouted and whistled for help. No one heard me. I rushed along deck, slipping, leaping, dodging obstructions as if by miracle. At last I reached the shelter of the cabin just as a fourth sea broke over the deck and washed across my knees.

"By this time the officer on watch had heard my calls. He was just on the point of going on the little bridge of the *Union* to ask what the matter was when the might of the sea, breaking on deck under his very feet, seized the bridge in its grasp, tore the whole structure loose, and washed it away. Had the officer been one step in advance he would have gone overboard to his death. As it was he saved himself by clinging to the cabin railing.

" 'Sir,' I panted when I got near him. 'The centre hatchway is open and filling with water.'

"He stood dumbfounded.

" 'The hatch open!' he gasped in a hoarse whisper. I could almost see his face pale in the darkness.

"Then his presence of mind returned. Rushing back into the cabin, he roused the crew and in a few minutes the whole tribe of us was on deck, working like devils to seal up the hatch. In our hurry we could find no ax and no tools. We worked with our bare fingers, seizing whatever came to hand and using it for our purpose. That night not one of us closed an eye. The work went on until the hatch was sealed. Then all of us sought shelter in the captain's cabin, leaving a watch on deck.

"I was just telling the men how Leers had been washed overboard when the door opened and the man himself stumbled in, hardly recognizable because of the blood and bruises on his head. The poor fellow, exhausted, had hardly strength enough to tell us what had happened to him.

"Seized by the sea in its wrath, he had been torn from his hold and dashed against the port bulwarks. As he fell a blow on his head had almost rendered him unconscious, but in the instant of fainting he remembered that if he should go to sleep he would be washed overboard and lost. By sheer will power he restored himself to consciousness and seized hold of the railing. Then, not daring to risk himself across the open deck, he had waited until he heard the shouting of the men, who were closing the middle hatchway. He thought that they were detailed to come to his rescue, warned of his condition by me. Too weak to call back to them, he waited in vain. At last, when all seemed to be quiet again, he had groped his way to us.

"We gave him some hot soup, bandaged his head, and put him to sleep in a corner. Hardly was he at rest when a second mariner came in to us carrying on his shoulder a soaked mattress. He had been waked in his sleep by the rushing of water about his bunk below decks and was forced to take shelter with us in the cabin. It was humorous to see him tote in the mattress. The thing was dripping wet and could of course afford no resting place. Nevertheless, he sat down on it with the sour remark that most likely we would all 'sleep a d—— sight wetter than that before morning.'

"In this mood we awaited the dawn, most of us ready for any eventuality, some of us not expecting to see daylight alive. The moaning and groaning of the coal slush in our hold, the howling of the wind above us in the rigging, the ceaseless thunder of the waves as they broke upon deck, all warned us each minute of an approaching end.

"It was with a cry of joy that we at last saw the first gray streaks of dawn. At once every man was on deck to see what was left of the *Union*. Some of us had verily expected that the ship would by this time be only a driving wreck. Yet despite the batterings of the night the old hulk still floated drunkenly about, the wasting waves regularly breaking over her.

"In the distance we beheld the *Kronprinz Wilhelm* riding high on the sea.

"Surely, we thought, now there will be no more need to leave us out here. For certainly Commander Thierfelder will send for us.

"This at first seemed the case. For a few minutes it looked as if the *Kronprinz Wilhelm* were bearing down to our rescue. We saw black smoke pour from her funnels and gave a shout of joy. The ship knew of our distress. She was coming to our rescue.

"But our hopes were soon blasted. The *Kronprinz Wilhelm* put on steam to the south, by degrees drawing farther and farther away until finally she was out of sight. Some of the men then began to swear; others only laughed. Our commanding officer, seeing our mood, called us together.

" 'Men,' he said, 'the *Kronprinz* has either sighted a ship or is being chased by a war vessel. In any case let us bravely wait out the day. And now all hands to the pumps! If we are to die let us die hard, like Germans. But I feel it in my blood that before night every man of us will be safe on board our ship again.' "

Chapter XI

THE "ANNE DE BRETAGNE" IS TAKEN AND THE CREW FISHES FOR ALBATROSS

THE men aboard the *Union* were deeply disappointed to see us steaming away toward the horizon. They could not see the ship we had sighted and did not know whether we were chasing or being chased. Commander Thierfelder had sent them wigwag signals from our bridge, but the message was obscured by the smoke from our funnels.

The *Kronprinz* was now bearing slowly in the direction of the sighted ship, hoping to save coal by not steaming too fast. The sailing vessel we were approaching, however, was of unusual speed and had a favourable wind, so that we soon had to increase our speed to a good clip. At 6:30 A. M. we reached the prize, a French three-masted bark of Nantes named the *Anne de Bretagne*.

Our prize crew at once got into its boat and rowed over to inspect the ship's papers and cargo. In contrast with the *Union* which had been sailing the seas for the last thirty years the *Anne de Bretagne* was a new vessel, only four years old. Her sails, however, were much patched and discoloured, and gave the ship an old and faded appear-

159

ance. Masts, spars, and bowsprit were painted white after the French fashion, while lower down the white bulwarks were set off by a dark hull painted red below the water line. The paint on the hull was parched and scaly, showing the ship at near view to disadvantage.

The *Anne de Bretagne's* cargo consisted of a load of lumber, which she was carrying from Fredrikstad, Norway, to Newcastle, Australia. This was not good news to us as lumber could obviously not be used as fuel.

The pretty French flag of the *Anne de Bretagne* was at once hauled down and her crew—twenty-six men in all—were taken aboard and lodged in the customary second-class prisoners' quarters. Among this crew were two Swedes and one Dane, all of whom could speak German. They at once set up a lively chatter with some of our crew in order to ingratiate themselves. Our men, however, were under orders not to communicate with them. Nevertheless, Scholke, our comedian—he of the round white face—knowing himself as immune from punishment as a court fool, began a loud conversation with the Dane, pretending to be the man's long-lost brother. Falling about the astonished stranger's neck, he held him tight, cried, told him how glad he was to see him again after all this time, and generally acted a genuine part.

At first the Dane in his astonishment began to protest. Then suddenly a change came over him. Thinking he had to do with a sincere man and expecting to win his way into the good graces of the ship by taking up the part, he now pretended to recognize a forgotten brother in Scholke. After a few moments' acting he proclaimed to the rest of us that Scholke was in truth his own long-lost brother. He now recognized him and was overjoyed to find him after so long a separation. At this the men could no longer contain their mirth and roars of laughter began to resound on the deck. The poor Dane was nonplussed.

Scholke had meanwhile also changed his tune and was now trying to persuade the Dane that he had made a mistake—that the Dane was only a former friend of his who owed him some money. Scholke now demanded payment of the money. It was side-splitting to see the comedian insist and the Dane angrily protest. The scene would have gone to even greater lengths if the crew which was to man the *Anne de Bretagne* had not just then been ordered over our side, temporarily putting an end to the fun. The Dane would have been teased for the rest of his stay on our ship if on the following day he had not felled one of the prisoners to the floor with a single wallop for jibing at him.

Twenty men of our crew went on board the captured bark to make everything ready, so that by one in the afternoon all was in order to get away. The towline, however, had yet to be attached—not an easy task, as it proved.

In fact, the making fast of this towline was now almost to cost us a life. A line attached to our towing cable was thrown over to the *Anne de Bretagne,* and a sailor named Joseph Zelinka, the same who had done such good service in the topmasts of the *Union* and who because of his mashed hand had been brought aboard our ship again to be sent over in turn to the new prize, ran out to the tip of the bowsprit to haul in the line. As the dare-devil did so he did not take into consideration the rapid warp to starboard which the *Anne de Bretagne* was taking. Hardly had he reached the tip of the bowsprit when his vessel and ours approached with a collision inevitable. Too late the men saw his danger. He must be crushed to death between the two vessels.

But Zelinka bore a charmed life. At the very instant of collision an intervening stroke of Providence raised the prow of the *Anne de Bretagne* on the crest of a wave. In a flash Zelinka saw his chance, leaped to our railing with the upward heave of the ship, and clambered out of reach just as the ships crashed together below him. The giant bowsprit upon which he had stood was broken in two pieces and bent hard to port, but the man was uninjured.

The line fastened, the bark was taken to tow. We now steamed in all haste back toward the *Union* which we knew we had left in bad straits. When we last saw her the bark had shown a list to starboard of some twenty to twenty-five degrees, while the seas seemed breaking over her decks, so that we were now asking ourselves whether she was still afloat and if not whether her men were safe in their boats. After four hours' steaming we again sighted the vessel which was now lying almost on her side.

In our haste to get to her we put our towline to too great a test. Hardly had we come up with the *Union* when this five-inch steel cable snapped in two. We did not then have time to repair it, so we let the *Anne de Bretagne* drift while we gave our attention to the helpless *Union*.

The little bark was indeed in a critical condition. Following a blustery night, the sea had been turbulent all day. The *Union,* lightened of so much coal and cargo, sat high in the water, lying as mentioned far over on her side. Despite the efforts of her brave crew at the pumps, there were already one and one half metres of water in her hold, and it was only a question of time before she must go to the bottom.

It was therefore imperative to get the exhausted men from her decks. Night was fast coming on and we believed the *Union* could hardly stay afloat until morning. Accordingly, despite the driving sea, our commander ordered the prize boat overboard to fetch the crew off. This boat at first pulled for the lee side of the bark which was her port. When it reached the *Union,* however, the men found the bark pitching and rolling in a dangerous manner. At any moment a heavy surge might throw the whole vessel over on the port side; such a movement would drown every man in the boat.

The prize crew, therefore, rowed away again and circled around to starboard, where after heroic efforts in the teeth of a heavy wind and a violent sea they came alongside the *Union.*

A desperate struggle to get the men off into the prize boat now began. As the little craft rose and fell and dashed against the sides of the *Union* her crew had to exert every effort to keep their boat from being shattered to bits. Meanwhile, the men on the *Union* clambered down the leaning vessel's side, watched their chance, and one by one leaped into the boat. The last man in was the commanding officer.

When all hands were off the *Union,* however, the troubles of the little boat seemed only begun, for, since it was on the windward side of the *Union,* both wind and waves were now uniting to drive it against the larger vessel. Indeed, it was doubtful whether the men would be able to get their boat away. Again and again they made the attempt but each time were driven savagely back against the *Union's* side. By persevering, however, they were finally rewarded luckily with a combined lurch of the vessel and heave of the sea; when, pulling as if possessed, they got away. Drenched to the skin and completely exhausted, they at last reached our side.

Every man was immediately given a glass of wine to revive his strength and some tobacco to reward his labours on the fated bark. The men from the *Union,* though overjoyed to get back, complained that they had been compelled to abandon all their reserve baggage, such as blankets and coats, on board the bark. We told them they were fortunate to get away with their lives.

That night there was festive rejoicing on board the

Kronprinz. The men from the *Union* recounted their adventures, each adding something from his imagination until quite a respectable narrative of truth and fable was gathered about the three-weeks' cruise aboard the bark. The two tales most liked were the closing of the hatch in the storm and the disappearance of the head from the figurehead of the vessel.

When Sunday, the twenty-second of November, dawned we expected to find the *Union* gone to the bottom, but the bark was still miraculously afloat, as if in despite of us and the ocean. Commander Thierfelder at once decided to send a crew over to her to make a final attempt to save those precious nine hundred tons of coal. A boat was dispatched at seven in the morning. Should the men succeed in getting upon the *Union's* decks they were to try to pump out her hold; and this despite the representations of the crew of the *Union* that the bark could not be pumped out. Should they fail in this, however, the men were at least to fetch back the trappings which they had left at the previous day's evacuation.

This boat soon reached the bark, but, try as it would, could not safely come alongside. For two hours it fought the sea, repeatedly trying to get near enough so that the men might board the *Union*. At last it gave up the attempt as too dangerous and put back to our side.

At eleven o'clock that day all hands were given their Sabbath holiday. A peculiar sport now began. It had been observed of late that despite the inclement weather our ship had been followed by great numbers of the albatross. This huge bird, the largest in fact of all aquatic birds, has a most singular appearance. When standing it resembles a monstrous duck, is a yard or more in height, and has yellow webbed feet lacking a hind toe, a long white body, and a back streaked or dusted with gray or brownish stripes. An elongated, strong beak is especially prominent and the upper mandible of this is hooked sharply downward at the end. When in flight the bird measures on the average about ten feet from wing tip to tip, though we saw some much larger—perhaps with an extension of fifteen to seventeen feet.

These birds followed our ship for days at a time, wheeling about in endless course, never tiring, apparently never resting from morning till night, and always keeping pace with us no matter what our speed. The sailors believe that the bird sleeps on the wing, and some are still in such superstitious awe of it that they can by no means be persuaded to kill one.

The peculiar downward hook of the upper beak and the bird's habit of alighting on the water to pick up any food that may be thrown overboard have given rise to a harmless sport—that of "painless" fishing for the albatross. Our crew indulged in this pastime this day and later on whenever the birds were around and the men were free from duty.

To catch the albatross special tackle was necessary. The purposeless cruelty of a hook was of course out of the question. A copper plate about four inches square and a sixteenth of an inch thick was sawed out so as to make a framework or hollow square, about three inches wide on the inside. To one corner of this plate were attached a few feet of wire and to this a long tough piece of twine. The two contiguous sides of the square frame opposite this corner were then baited with sufficient pork to make the whole buoyant enough to float. The baited plate, thrown over-board, drifted from the ship and was ready for its vic-tim.

No sooner did an albatross see food than it glided down to the water and swam up to the bait. The sailor meanwhile watched his chance. All depended on his being ready at the proper instant.

The albatross, as above stated, has a bill sharply bent downward at the end so as to form a veritable hook. The instant it seized the bait the sailor pulled on the line. This caused the hook of the bill to catch on the baited copper plate so that the bird could not let loose so long as the sailor pulled on the line. The man therefore kept the line taut by pulling rapidly hand over hand until the huge bird was safely towed up the side of the ship into his arms.

Once on deck and a captive, the albatross would duck its head about, make frantic efforts to escape, and look par-ticularly foolishly at heaven, sea, and guffawing crew. Finding itself a captive, it then immediately proceeded to get seasick, partly, perhaps, from fright, partly from the unsteady motion of the vessel, and vomited lustily to right and left.

At this stage of the sport the bird was again turned loose, when with loud cheers from the crew and an anxious squawk from the albatross the bird would fly swiftly away to be caught all over again later in the same manner.

This harmless sport kept the crew in the best of humour and was, in fact, a good exercise in alertness. Often, however, in a different mood, those of the men who scorned superstition used the flying albatross as a target, shooting at it for practice. The killings, despite Coleridge's legend of the mariner with the glittering eye, did not bring our ship any ill luck of which we were aware. They did, however, furnish supper to many a hungry brother albatross which cannibal-wise seized upon its luckless kin as soon as the life was out.

I could not look upon these birds without trying to think of some way in which to get a pair of them back to Europe alive. It will be remembered that the late Queen Victoria offered a prize of one million dollars for a living pair brought to England. A ship equipped with ice to maintain a temperature at which the bird might live was fitted out, but it returned without living specimens, all having died on the way to England.

On a trip some years before I shot a few specimens, treated their skins with tobacco, and brought them home. The largest specimen, which was later mounted and now rests over the doorway of my home in Poland, measures

The ANNE DE BRETAGNE, *a French bark carrying lumber, resisted firing, ramming, and a charge of dynamite, and was left finally, a shattered derelict.*

Lieutenant "NIEZY" (left) with CHARLES KRAUSE, *American customs officer, and Lieutenant* HEINZ HOFFMANN, *taken on the arrival of the* KRONPRINZ *at Newport News, April 11, 1915.*

twelve feet three inches from tip to tip. The peasants, seeing the hooked beak of the bird, spread the report that it was an American eagle, but I learned that our family servants had encouraged the report, adding that the bird was a deadly enemy to man, gave battle on sight, and usually conquered its antagonist. This embellishment was of course intended to redound to my glory in shooting the bird.

While some of the holiday-making crew were thus busy catching and teasing the stupid albatross, a cry went up suddenly that the *Union* was sinking. All hands at once went to our port rail to view the vessel. It was a false alarm, however, for, though the bark was lying far over on her side, rolling and plunging like a toy, she had not yet begun to sink. At 3 P. M. the alarm was sounded again, and once more all hands crowded the rail. This time the bark had listed still farther to starboard, her masts making an angle of thirty degrees with the water. There was now no question that she must soon go down, for she was gradually filling. All hands therefore stood by to await the end.

As expected, at about 4 P. M. the fated vessel suddenly lay completely over on her side, rapidly filled, and at 4:15 P. M. disappeared under the surface. The *Union* had sailed her last sea.

A great quantity of wood, cork life belts, life buoys, rope, and sailcloth floated over the spot. These articles, found by an Allied vessel, might give a clue to our whereabouts, so two boats were sent out to fish them up.

Sunday, given over to rest and pleasure, was followed by a Monday full of serious work. The *Anne de Bretagne* floated gracefully a ship's length away, and as much of her cargo as would be of use to us had yet to be removed. We had also to bear in mind that at any minute another prize might come in sight or a warship as fast as the *Kronprinz* steam down from the horizon.

Whatever our anxiety to begin, however, we nevertheless had to wait until the sea should become calmer. At one in the afternoon we brought the *Anne de Bretagne* on our port and took on provisions, wine, sailcloth, baggage, paint, and a winch. Three living pigs, protesting as their predecessors had at being hoisted upon deck, helped make up this potpourri.

At 5 P. M., when we had taken out all of her usable cargo and our crew had once more come aboard us, we let go the bark and stood off to port, whereupon the order "Clear for action!" sounded. The *Anne de Bretagne* was to be attacked for practice.

We now steamed about two miles away, then turned around and again made for the bark. At four thousand metres our two guns began shooting twenty-two rounds apiece, sixteen shell and six incendiary. At six hundred metres our machine gun opened fire, being immediately followed by the rifles of our sharpshooters. The noise and the smoke together with the trembling of the ship at once threw the men into the mood of real action. It was inspiring to see with what enthusiasm and precision the

crews worked. Even down in the engine- and fireroom the
men worked as if the fate of the ship depended on the
outcome of the manœuvre.

The shooting was as good as we had expected. The bark
showed important hits and was on fire forward. The
blaze was soon extinguished, however, by lack of air and
the presence in the hold of much water which the vessel
had shipped during the last few days.

Despite our good shooting, the *Anne de Bretagne* sank
but little, her cargo of wood, imprisoned below decks, keeping her afloat. It would be necessary to blow out her side
with dynamite or to ram her until she went down. We
thought it best to try ramming.

At seven-thirty in the evening we steamed down upon
the bark at half speed, intending to cut her in two, amidships. There was a tremendous crash, a tremor went
through our ship, but when we backed away the *Anne de
Bretagne* was still afloat. Three times we tried to cut the
vessel in two, but still the bark obstinately held together.
At the fourth ramming our own ship began to leak. The
plates of our prow had buckled, the seams opened, and it
was necessary to close the forward compartments.

Foiled in our attempt at ramming, but especially desirous
to destroy the bark, we sent a boat over to dynamite her.
Our men placed charges in the bow and one at the mainmast, set the fuses, and rowed away. A spectacular explosion followed, sending a shower of débris into the air,
but when the smoke cleared away, though the bow of the

Anne was shattered, the mainmast still stood intact. This mast in fact was of hollow steel 135 feet high, the metal being 10 mm. thick, which accounted for its sturdiness. In the afternoon we again planted charges, one at the poop, the other at the mainmast. Again the result was the same. The mainmast stood and the ship, though completely filled with water, was kept afloat by her cargo of wood.

Once more we tried ramming, but now a new danger presented itself, for the force of our collision caused the now weakened mainmast to sway over our deck. We held our breath, expecting it to fall, but it stayed in place. Had it fallen it would have shattered our bridge. This dangerous experiment could not be repeated, so we stood off until midnight, hoping to see the mainmast fall as a result of the pitching of the vessel. But when at that hour the mast still held up its head, we gave the *Anne de Brentagne* into the care of Neptune and left her, a driving derelict upon the wind-swept sea.

For the next week we settled down to routine and repair work. As our prow leaked badly as a result of the fruitless ramming of the *Anne de Bretagne,* we pumped out the forepeak and filled it solid with concrete. This not only stopped the leaks: it served as an effective protection against further damage to our prow in case we should have to resort to ramming in future.

On Wednesday, the twenty-fifth of November, as we were steaming along at sixteen miles an hour, we sighted a sail three points to the north. At once the men had hopes of a chase. The commander did not consider the prize important enough to interrupt the repair work, so we kept our course. At 3 P. M. we sighted a second sail which we also passed by without molesting.

By the end of the week, however, officers, crew, and ship had sufficiently recuperated from the experiences with the *Union* and the *Anne de Bretagne* and all were ready for game. Hoffmann was particularly anxious to see action.

"Niezy," he asked me one morning as we had breakfast together, "what do you think the end of this whole business is going to be? Do you, in the bottom of your heart, believe we're going to get safely through the war; or do you think, deep down in your soul, that we won't live through it? Every man has a feeling about things like that. What is yours?"

"I'm sure, Heinz," I answered, "I haven't the slightest idea."

"Come," he urged, "I mean this as between us. What do you think, deep down in your heart, is going to be the end of all this?"

"Really, Heinz," I answered, "I have to turn down my glass. I haven't any conviction one way or another. You know my position on this ship. If Germany wins the war, where then is Poland? If the Allies win, what will Russia do for Poland?" (The events on the *Kronprinz Wilhelm* happened before the Russian revolution.) "As for me, when I look into the future I look into the night."

He was quiet a moment, then he faced me and spoke musingly.

"Something tells me, Niezy, that you'll get back home again all right. You're just that kind of a lucky dog—you nobleman, you. But as for me, middle-class offshoot, something tells me I'll never see home again."

I could not suppress a laugh.

"Something's wrong with your digestion—that's all."

He shrugged his shoulders.

"If I get to the other world before you do—— Hello!" he cried. "There goes the gong. We've sighted another ship."

Chapter XII

THE RITUAL OF LINE BAPTISM

WHEN we came on deck ready for action, we saw on the horizon a steamer with one smokestack, evidently a good prize. The *Kronprinz* at a speed of eighteen miles hove down on the vessel. In a short time we began to make out the marks of a Dutchman, so, the neutral identity established, we cut down our speed and allowed the steamer to disappear.

Now, craving indulgence, I shall here take up the story of the jolly Line Baptism, which, some time ago, I promised to tell at an opportune time.

It will be remembered that when the *Kronprinz Wilhelm* was first about to cross the equator on her southerly course there were aboard her some seventy men who had never before crossed the line. And these men according to seaman's rule had to be baptized to the sea before they could be permitted to cross to the Southern Hemisphere.

For the last two or three days, in fact, all green men on board had been receiving warnings that something dire would soon happen to them. These warnings were not unlike those received by candidates for degrees in secret orders, the old hands betting the new ones cigars, wine, etc., that they would get killed in the ordeal, while the green men asked their experienced friends for further particulars.

Meanwhile, the seasoned sailors were getting things ready. Old pieces of rope were unravelled to make hempen hair or Hottentot skirts for some of the actors, while other seamen were to be seen sitting on the lee decks cutting out and painting paper clothes or fashioning of wood a Neptune's tripod, a monstrous razor, canes, a sextant, and a Bible.

The day before the ceremony, when everything else was ready, some of the crew stretched out from rail to cabin on the port promenade deck a piece of tarpaulin about twenty feet square in such manner as to form a tank, and filling it with water to detect leaks, left it filled and stationed a guard to prevent the novices from slashing holes in it and so frustrating the ceremonies. In this tank the green men were to be baptized.

Over the bow side of the tank a barrel hoop was suspended by means of a rope, the hoop being wound with cloth to prevent its scratching the naked candidates, who should soon be shoved through it.

At last the ominous morning arrived. At nine o'clock the actors—all experienced men—assembled at the tank and held a parley. There stood Neptune, robed in black, a cardboard crown upon his head, and in his hand a wooden trident—Neptune, god of the festival. Beside him stood his wife, a slender seaman whose hempen hair fell as low as his knees, and at her side the wife of the pastor, also a seaman in lady's attire. The latter held her arms locked with those of her pious husband, who, gowned in solemn black with white collar, smoked eyeglasses, and shovel hat, inclined his face toward heaven and pressed against his stomach a Bible made of two pieces of plank hinged together along one edge—it was painted black and inscribed with a silver cross.

Behind this trio came the master of ceremonies, a tall man of stern mien, half hidden under a hat of painted cardboard two feet high. Near him was the squatty barber, who held before him a wooden razor three feet long. A learned doctor of medicine, an astronomer, and a herd of husky seamen, naked save for a Hottentot's garb of rope about their loins and all besmeared with coal dust or burnt cork, completed the group.

After an important parley an agreement was reached to the effect that there was on board the *Kronprinz* a large number of landsmen covered with the filth and grime of landsmen's existence. They were polluting the pure ship, and now that the latter was about to cross the line this unfortunate condition could not continue. Before Jove and by Neptune, it must be remedied at once.

"Most high and mighty Neptune," the pastor began, addressing the wearer of the pasteboard crown. "Gracious and renowned sir: Bearing in mind these complaints of our valiant crew, your loyal and most faithful worshippers, what shall be done?"

At this Neptune raised himself to his full height and thumped his wooden trident upon the deck.

"These men shall be cleansed of their earthly dust by the baptism!" he thundered. "Our will be done!"

"Amen!" answered the pastor.

"Amen!" echoed the crew.

"Let us begin at once," the master of ceremonies directed.

The signal given, the men began to move, when suddenly as if on inspiration the pastor again stepped forward.

"Gracious and most mighty lord," he said in a pious and solemn voice, "were it not well first to ask permission of the commander of the good ship *Kronprinz Wilhelm,* before we put his crew through the baptism?"

"Well said!" spoke the master of ceremonies.

"Well said!" the crew echoed, thumping on the deck in approbation.

Hereupon Neptune again addressed himself to his following:

"We, Neptune, all ruler of the sea, what lives thereon, therein, or thereunder; we, omnipotent Neptune, command that the commander of the good ship *Kronprinz Wilhelm* be asked permission to let his crew undergo the baptism. Let it be done!"

The procession now moved on, at its head Neptune in stately step, escorted by his wife on one side and the redoubtable master of ceremonies on the other. Behind them in equal pace marched the pastor and his wife; then in due order came the doctor, the astronomer, their wives and ladies, and a rout of Hottentots, beating drums, tooting horns, and uttering war whoops, intended to make the unbaptized members of the crew, in hiding below decks, quake for their lives.

Slowly, magnificently, the procession passed forward, around in front of the commander's bridge, then astern on the starboard side, and finally back to its original position. Here the Hottentots at a signal from the master of ceremonies detached themselves to go in search of the hiding heathen, while the rest continued to the bridge.

At the port stairway the procession formed in double file, and then the solemn tramp upon the brass-plated steps kept time to the thud of the drum as the stately band slowly mounted to the bridge. Before the men reached the top they were stopped by the master of ceremonies. This imposing wizard now went in advance to see whether the officers were on the bridge. Of course, knowing what was to happen, they were all present, so the master of ceremonies returned and advised Neptune that everything was ready. Whereupon the procession mounted and took its place on the bridge.

The master of ceremonies now walked up before Commander Thierfelder who was expecting him, and taking off his top-heavy hat made a deep bow.

"Most valiant Commander," he said, "we, the rulers of Neptune's realm; after due investigation and proper Neptonic certification, finding upon your best of ships the polluting traces of unbaptized landsmen—being about to cross the sanctified line which no heathen durst ever do— beg in the name of Neptune and the rest that no unbaptized seaman be longer tolerated on the good ship *Kronprinz Wilhelm;* wherefore by leave of our most mighty sea god we crave your Highness's permission to wash from the unsanctified limbs and bodies of that unsacrosanct part of Your Highness's crew their landish dust. Most valiant sir, what is your gracious pleasure?"

At the conclusion of this speech Commander Thierfelder heaved a genuine sigh.

"Oh," he said as if relieved, "I thought you wanted to hold an execution or something, but if that's all you want, go right ahead."

In reply the master of ceremonies bowed as deeply as before.

"But," continued Commander Thierfelder, "is Neptune certain that we are about to cross the line? Has his assistant made his observation of the heavens?"

In answer the master of ceremonies turned toward his followers.

"Astronomer," he commanded sternly, "stand forth!"

The astronomer at once came from behind the shelter of Neptune's back. In his hand he bore a wooden sextant.

"Astronomer," the master of ceremonies repeated, "present your credentials."

"Most worthy Master," the astronomer answered, "my credentials are here in this sextant, the most accurate of its kind, and above in the stars, the most glorious of their kind. He who believes, may he prosper; and he who doubts, may he be hit by a shooting star."

"Enough!" thundered the master of ceremonies stamping his foot. "We recognize you as the one and only astronomer upon Neptune's ocean able to tell to a hair's breadth whether the good ship *Kronprinz Wilhelm* is crossing the line. Proceed to the measurements of the heavens and tell the worthy commander of the *Kronprinz Wilhelm* whether we have reached the line."

The astronomer accordingly turned to Commander Thierfelder.

"Most mighty Commander," he began, making a reverential bow, "we crave your leave and pardon, here on the bridge of the good ship *Kronprinz Wilhelm,* to shoot the sun."

"Shoot!" answered Commander Thierfelder.

Hereupon the astronomer held his sextant before him, mumbled a few charms, raised the clumsy instrument to his eye and solemnly shot the sun. Then lowering it again, he solemnly proclaimed:

"All ye who believe in the stars of the heavens and their mother, the sea, attend! 'Tis high noon and on the bosom of the ocean, and by accurate measurement we, astronomer of the god of the sea, find the good ship *Kronprinz Wilhelm* to be crossing the line."

Commander Thierfelder looked surprised, took out his watch, shook his head as if disagreeing, and then turned with a shrug of his shoulders to Neptune.

"If you're satisfied——" he said, finishing with a shrug.

The astronomer, his office done, stepped back again

behind Neptune, while the master of ceremonies came forward.

"In the name of Neptune, gracious sir, most humble thanks. But will it not please Your Honour to witness the solemn baptism of your now-to-be-blessed-forever crew?"

"Certainly," Commander Thierfelder responded. "With the greatest of pleasure. . . . Lieutenants Fix and Rüderbusch, take command of the bridge, and the rest of you"—addressing the other officers—"stay here with the lieutenants and keep a sharp lookout for the enemy while I go to watch the crew get baptized."

He was about to go forward when the undaunted master of ceremonies stepped in his way.

"Most gracious lord," he said. "Most honoured ruler of the good ship *Kronprinz Wilhelm,* it were a great shame to leave behind so goodly a company of officers of His Majesty's navy. Will it not please the gallant commander to let all the officers on the watch come with you to witness the ceremonies?"

"But what if the enemy should come up? The lookout in the crow's nest may at any minute sight a sail, and off to port there is a haze that looks like smoke. That might be an enemy cruiser."

"Baptism before all things earthly," answered the diplomatic master of ceremonies. "I, wizard of Neptune's realm and especially of this his baptismal procession, do command all enemies of the *Kronprinz Wilhelm* to stay away until the ceremony is over."

"All right," answered the good-natured commander. "With this assurance on your part I am willing to proceed."

"Thanks!" said the master of ceremonies, bowing.

"Amen," wheezed the pastor.

"Amen," echoed the crew.

At a nod from the master of ceremonies the drum struck up, and the procession descended to the promenade deck, where it retraced its steps to the water tank.

Here the expected pantomime awaited them. For the grotesque figures of the Hottentot aides of Neptune stood ranged in a line, each holding fast to a captive heathen. The victims had been pulled from their places of hiding, some from ship's boats, some from the masthead, others from the bunkers, and they were now casting wistful glances at a pot of liquid tar which one of the Hottentots kept stirring suggestively with a paint brush—the barber's lather and shaving brush.

We officers were shown to chairs provided for us, and the bulk of the crew took places about deck and on the railing.

Neptune's followers now gathered about their king in a semicircie, whereupon the master of ceremonies made a bow to Commander Thierfelder.

"Most worthy Commander," he said, "in humble deference we ask your leave to begin."

Commander Thierfelder nodded, whereupon Neptune turned to his following.

"It is our will and pleasure," he said, "that this ever-memorable baptism begin."

"Amen," repeated the master of ceremonies.

"Amen," echoed the crew.

The pastor now came to the front with his wooden Bible, opened to two hinged pieces of plank, and solemnly read a service. Then he raised his eyes to heaven, his voice to the funnel tops, and preached a sermon, after which he blessed the poor victims and hoped almighty Jove would bring them through the ceremony safe and sound.

The worthy doctor now came forward followed by his assistants, each of whom carried a water bucket filled with pills. These pills were plums from which the seeds had been removed and replaced with spiced oil.

The first landsman was now dragged into the centre of the semicircle. It happened to be a certain Miller. Miller was lifted astride a plank, placed across two barrels, and then the doctor took him by the ear.

"Miller," he thundered, "open your mouth and let me feel your pulse. Let me hear your heart. Aha! I find you are suffering from a serious disease. An X-ray is not necessary. You lack one lung, have a treacherous taste for strong drink, and cannot withstand the pipe and the cards. And, before I forget it, I see that your brains have turned to sponge. Wherefore, O Miller, I prescribe for you seven pills from the pill boxes in the pharmacy of Neptune."

At these words Miller tried to bolt but was held fast by three Hottentots. His mouth was forced open and the first

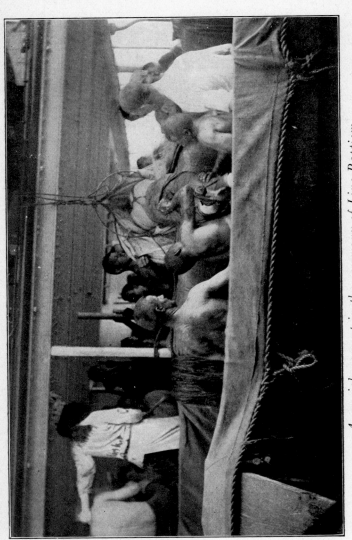

A crucial moment in the ceremony of Line Baptism.

oiled plum shoved down. Miller squirmed and gasped but all to no purpose. One by one the plums were rolled down his throat, one strong hand pulling his nose upward while a second held his chin downward.

At last the medicine was administered. Miller made a tragic face, felt his stomach, and fell to swearing in quite unbaptismal manner.

"Hold!" cried the doctor. "I begin to fear I have overlooked that Miller is also suffering from wind in the vocabulary. Wherefore I administer one pill more."

Alas! Miller had to swallow this one too. But, O Miller, it is not all over—it has only begun for you.

"I'm satisfied," said the doctor, "that as a result of my good prescription Miller is on the road to recovery. Miller, I demand my fee."

"It shall be paid you," the master of ceremonies answered for Miller. "Barber, step forth and shave Miller of his landsman's filth."

"With pleasure and at once," grumbled the barber, stepping forth with his three-foot razor. In a trice an assistant brought up the bucket of tar. The barber ceremoniously took out the paint brush dripping with the sticky liquid and began to lather poor naked Miller from head to foot. The man danced, squirmed, and sputtered, but the Hottentots held him tightly. Then the barber took his wooden razor in both hands as an American baseball batter holds a bat, and scraped the tar from Miller, spattering handfuls of the wipings overboard into the sea.

"Lord of the Sea," he reported, "I, barber to Your Highness, affirm on bended knee that this heathen Miller is shaved of his landsman's filth and is ready for baptism."

Neptune nodded, whereupon the master of ceremonies raised his hand.

"Baptize him!" he commanded.

Four husky Hottentots at once seized Miller, raised him to the height of the tank, and, his tarry body squirming, tossed him like any clown in the circus through the cloth-wound hoop head-foremost into the tank. Here the lusty Hottentots ducked him until they thought he had had enough. He was then commanded to lower his head reverentially while the pastor pronounced the benediction.

"I, pastor of Neptune," he ended solemnly, "here proclaim thee a new-born follower of the sea, and thy name hereafter shall be 'Canned Salmon.' Arise, Canned Salmon, and salute your brothers!"

Then as Canned Salmon raised his head the crew shouted him welcome in his new name. He was now allowed to vault out of the tank. But his life was not yet safe. For the hose leading from the ship's pumps which had been feeding the tank was at once played upon the poor fellow until he had collected his senses and dashed out of range.

All this had proceeded under the lustiest guffaws of officers and men. Miller disposed of, the next man was brought forward and the process repeated. This time it was Rothmeyer. The doctor proclaimed that Rothmeyer was suffering from marriageitis in twenty ports, lacked all sense of distinction between good and bad cigars, had neither a full purse nor an empty stomach, was nothing, had always been nothing, and would become nothing unless he straightway took some sovereign pills which would at once restore him to celibacy, bring back his sense of distinction in matters tobacconic, fill his purse, empty his stomach, and in short make something of him.

Rothmeyer who had learned nothing from Miller's experience also struggled against captivity. He was consequently declared too full-blooded, for which additional ailment he must receive ten pills to thin his blood. Poor Rothmeyer then went through the performance which Miller had undergone and was finally baptized "Redheaded Whale." Then came the turn of the steward named Ostertager. And so on down the line.

The officers laughed, the crew shouted jokes and taunts, and fun reigned. As the end of the baptismal line was neared all parties had become physically as well as emotionally tired, so that the last men were put through hurriedly, getting off more easily. They were dosed only a pill apiece, were given a hasty lathering, scraping, and ducking, and quickly scrambled out of reach of the hose.

When all were baptized the pastor blessed the performance, hoping it might be as successful next time. The master of ceremonies then announced that Neptune would hold a ball that night, and after thanking the commander and his officers for their kind attendance and excellent behaviour, disbanded the procession.

The officers went back to their quarters, Neptune and his Hottentots disappeared below decks, and the tarred-up novitiates stood about, oiling and scraping themselves and each other, trying to get off the tarry lather of which they would not be entirely free for days to come.

That evening more of the crew dressed up as women, chose partners, and appeared at the ball which was held in the officer's mess room. The ship's band played and all danced. Each received a bottle of beer and some cigars—the women, of course, smoking and drinking as courageously as their partners—and gayety held sway.

Toward the middle of the ball the commander was asked to give out diplomas to the new-born followers of Neptune, so he made a short speech and bestowed upon each newly baptized man a diploma which, printed upon the back side of a former ship's menu card, read as follows:

S. M. AUXILIARY CRUISER "KRONPRINZ WILHELM"
WAR EMERGENCY BAPTISMAL DIPLOMA

We, Neptune, ruler over all flowing and standing waters that exist—oceans, washbowls, frog and duck ponds, puddles and public bathing pools—have found ourselves inclined to grant to the miserable landsman:

F. FEHLKAMM

the high favour of a War Emergency Line Baptism, after (he had been) cleaned, scraped, and scratched of the horror-engendering filth of the Northern territories according to the ceremony of the all-highest secret chief of the Nautical Barber and Friseur Department.

We have therefore resolved to take up the latter into the ranks of the vassals and servants of our watery kingdom under the name of "Carp." We herewith authorize our whole courtly following and servants, from shark to oyster, from full-bosomed mermaid to the sharp-bellied old fogy of the sea, to let this creature pass unhindered in all places and at all hours.

Given at the equator, 33 degrees west longitude, the second of September, 1914, on board the S. M. Auxiliary Cruiser *Kronprinz Wilhelm.*

Certified by my signature and seal.

NEPTUNE.

The bestowal of these passes completed, the dance commenced again. As the hours advanced, one by one the crew stole off to bed, and the crowd dwindled. At midnight the electric lights went out and the remaining revellers were forced to grope their way below decks.

I began my watch at that hour and the bridge seemed desolate after the gayety of the evening. I could not help reflecting how completely the serious mission of the *Kronprinz Wilhelm* had been forgotten in the revelries of the day, and what a strange sensation it would be if now, as the men stretched their tired bones on their bunks, the ship's gong should sound suddenly "Clear for action!"

Chapter XIII

THE "BELLEVUE" CARRIES A DIVERTING CARGO

AT five-thirty on the morning of December 4th I was roused from my bunk by the call "Clear for action!" A fair-sized steamer was on the horizon, which as we came nearer we made out to be the English steamer *Bellevue* of Glasgow—evidently a good prize.

The name *Bellevue,* meaning a "beautiful view," seemed auspicious and led us to wonder what the ship would have in her hold. This question was soon answered.

The *Bellevue* came to a halt at our command, surrendered, and gave up her papers to our prize crew which had immediately been dispatched to her. Her cargo consisted of two thousand eight hundred tons of cargo coal, one thousand tons of bunker coal, large quantities of machine parts packed in boxes, tons of gun metal, two automobiles with extra parts (especially spare wheels), twelve live oxen, a plentiful supply of beautifully dyed wool, and a rich cellar of wines and whisky. The coal was an important capture, for we needed it badly; the machine and automobile parts were also a useful acquisition; the oxen as well as the beautiful wool were, under the circumstances, not to be despised; but our crew considered the wine and the whisky the best part of the spoils.

Curiously enough, we discovered that the automobiles were intended for a German firm in La Plata. We thus saw that British business sense was not drawing patriotic lines. The "Lime-eaters," as our men called them, might fight the "Dutchman" in Europe, but they were not averse to doing business with him at the same time in South America. Our men talked about this for some time.

Officers and crew of the steamer—thirty-three in all—were ordered aboard the *Kronprinz*, where they were given the usual second-class quarters. The prisoners already quartered there from the *Union* and the *Anne de Bretagne* welcomed the newcomers cordially and fraternized with them in their common misfortune. Some seemed to regard the whole business as a good joke; others were incensed over their detention; still others merely shrugged their shoulders, looked cynically content, and confined themselves to borrowing tobacco and playing cards. The captured officers distinguished themselves by holding aloof from the men. Among themselves, however, they were quite sociable.

Our second division soon went aboard the *Bellevue* to man the steamer, but hardly were these men on board when again our alarm sounded. The lookout had descried a funnel some points to port. Luck was falling fast upon the *Kronprinz;* the sighted steamer gave evidence of being a prize.

It was nine-fifteen in the morning and a bright sun

sparkled over the sea. The enemy, therefore, would have a clear view of us. In fifteen minutes preparations for leaving the *Bellevue* had been rushed to conclusion and we set out at full speed after the prize.

To catch her was not to be so easy. At nine-thirty the steamer recognized us and showed that she was not going to wait calmly for us to come up. Turning about, she put on all steam, pouring as much black smoke over her stern as if she were a destroyer making a smoke screen. It was not long, however, before she was forced to recognize that we were the faster vessel and must overtake her.

Meanwhile, she was using her wireless to call for help. Lieutenant Brinkmann, who was waiting for this, at once began sparking in between with his powerful set, rendering the enemy's message unintelligible.

This wireless duel continued for an hour until we came within range, when the enemy, seeing the hopelessness of further flight, surrendered.

The captured steamer bore the name *Mont Agel*. She was a trim, newly built vessel of about five thousand tons, her hull red below the water line, sea-gray above, her cabin white, and her yellow funnel encircled with a broad white band. Our prize crew at once rowed over to her, to learn that the ship, which of all the ships had made the greatest effort to escape, was in ballast. One pig, one ox, and six sheep, together with a handful of provisions, was all she had on board. The animals were killed on the spot, as we had reason to believe they had been poisoned when the ship surrendered.

The wireless outfit, however, was no small acquisition. Though of the French system and very primitive, it was later on to prove of service to Lieutenant Brinkmann in deceiving the enemy.

The transfer of luggage and crew to our decks at once began. By 1 P. M. everything of value was aboard and the vessel ready to be sent to the bottom. Our seacock crew accordingly opened the ship's cocks. The *Mont Agel,* however, sank slowly. This was the more exasperating; first, as we wanted to get back to the *Bellevue;* and, second, as we knew that, with all the wireless disturbances our two ships had made, enemy vessels must have suspected the cause and now be speeding in our direction. There was no time to lose.

Accordingly, we steamed away a short distance, turned about, and rammed the *Mont Agel* amidships, first on the port, then on the starboard, each time with force enough to sink an ordinary ship. But the newness of the vessel was saving her; she kept sturdily afloat.

Again we rammed her, this time in the stern and with such force that we tore a broad hole in her side through which the water rushed like a brook. So fast did she now sink that I had time to take only three pictures at intervals of a minute before she disappeared.

Before the ship had gone down, however, a heart-rending

scene took place. I said that when we opened the seacocks of the *Mont Agel* we had taken off every living thing. This included two dogs, several cats, and some canaries. One cat, however, had somehow been overlooked. Not until the ship was rammed for the last time did the animal appear, when it jumped through the aft skylight and ran bounding over the deck, mewing loudly, perfectly conscious of its danger.

What was to be done? After the last crash we had backed too far away to give aid and the ship was going down rapidly. To send a boat over to the *Mont Agel* would have been sure death to its occupants, as the craft would have arrived only in time to be sucked down in the vortex of the sinking ship.

In this moment of excitement Karl Sturm, our erstwhile stowaway from the *Walhalla,* came rushing up to the bridge.

"Captain," he panted, "if you can steam over near, the men can let me down by a rope. I can get her." He could not stand seeing the animal go down.

Commander Thierfelder shook his head, at which the boy looked quite pained.

The *Mont Agel,* in fact, was by this time nearly under the water. Even as young Sturm was begging to save the animal, the boilers of the doomed vessel, chilled and fractured by the cold sea water which poured in around them, blew up with a tremendous crash, and when the smoke and steam cleared away neither cat nor ship was to be seen.

This whole incident into which such an array of emotion had centred after we discovered the unfortunate cat had taken less time than its telling. When it was over we faced about and put on all steam toward the *Bellevue* which, according to orders, had got under way and was slowly coming up. When we reached her at six o'clock everything was running smoothly. It was too late in the evening, however, to do any unloading, especially as we wanted to get away from the neighbourhood, so we ordered the *Bellevue* to follow us, put on twelve miles' steam, and cruised toward the northeast.

That night we were doubly watchful for danger. We regarded these waters off the coast of Brazil as particularly perilous; at any moment we might expect to sight an Allied war vessel. To take no chances, Commander Thierfelder doubled the guard which stood at the guns all night ready for trouble. Nothing happened, however, and morning broke with no enemy in sight.

For two days the *Bellevue* followed in our wake. On the second, a Sunday, all hands were assembled on our poop and addressed by the commander who thought the moment appropriate for reinspiring the crew.

He spoke of our prolonged stay on shipboard. Up to the present the discipline and readiness of the men to duty had been excellent. Despite trial of every kind, each had done his work without murmuring, conscientiously, patriotically. One was reminded of the gallant work of the little crew aboard the *Union*. For these endured hardships the Fatherland would one day reward them with gratitude and honour.

We were now entering upon a week of hard work, nay, even of drudgery. In the hold of the *Bellevue* were three thousand tons of coal which must be taken over. Coaling is not child's play, as everyone knows, and after so much of it all hands were indeed sick of the very sight of coal; but, let it be remembered, the continued freedom of the ship, the safety, nay, the life of every man on board, depended upon our having a good supply.

Let every man then do his duty as before, submitting himself to present trial that future good might come. As for his men, the commander felt in his heart every day more keenly the worth of their gallant German courage, perseverance, and zeal.

This speech, which was greeted with prolonged cheers, served its purpose, for the men were visibly in better mood. At 11 A. M. all hands were given a holiday, each man receiving as a bonus a glass of wine from the casks of the erstwhile *Union*.

On Monday the sea was too restless for the *Bellevue* to be taken alongside, so she followed in our wake, while our men went through military drill. Our crew on the *Bellevue* had discovered that the Englishmen had opened the valves to the water tanks and boilers, so that all fresh water on board had run into the sea. As our own supply was too small to allow of our sparing any, the *Bellevue* thenceforth had to use salt water in her boilers.

On Tuesday the sea had calmed down considerably, so we took the *Bellevue* on our port and began unloading. It was necessary first to throw overboard large quantities of her cargo of gun metal as this stood in the way of the coal. This audacious waste roused the criticism of some of our men who, being Germans of the economical type, did not like to see the loss of the valuable material. I, too, could not help thinking how useful this same metal would be on land.

"It's a big waste," I said to Hoffmann who stood beside me at the rail.

"Yes," he answered. "When I see all these ships and cargoes go to the bottom, I have to think how well I could establish myself with only a little of them if I had them in my possession at home. I could be rich. Then Heinz would not have to look far for a wife. But the sea gets it all."

"Let's go up to the Wiener Kaffee," he added. "You're off duty."

No sooner suggested than done, so, locking arms, we mounted the stairway.

The Wiener Kaffee was a comfortable room upon the boat deck between the third and fourth funnels in which we officers sought rest and refreshment. Here, over pleasant little tables, wine, cakes, and comfits were to be had, and a man could stretch his legs, puff his cigarette, or chat to his heart's content.

That afternoon, as the unloading of the *Bellevue* continued, Hoffmann and I spent some hours together. I want especially to speak of our conversation because of the strange dénouement.

Hoffmann, in brief, had had a strange dream the night before and he did not know whether to be troubled or amused.

"I thought that I was on the bridge on watch, when suddenly I saw the sky light up in the west. Soon I beheld two squadrons of warships bearing down on each other at tremendous speed. It was a German squadron and a British. Suddenly the British guns began to flash and the Germans' answered.

"Then a running fight took place and the whole sea was lit up with exploding shells. I stood at the rail and shouted to the German squadron to blow the British squadron off the sea, when suddenly to my horror the German ships themselves all blew up at the same instant. Then I reached out my hand to help a sinking sailor climb on board, and who do you think it was?"

"Can't guess," I answered.

"You," he said. "For some strange reason I was not a bit surprised. I pulled you out of the sea and then woke up."

I chuckled over this dream, as superstitions do not trouble me. But I could see that the dream worried Hoffmann. He became quiet after a while, letting me do most of the talking, and though I left him with a joke on my lips I had the feeling that the good fellow was not happy. He was probably homesick.

What was my astonishment when that very evening Brinkmann told us in private that a naval engagement had taken place off the Falkland Islands. A squadron of German cruisers under Admiral von Spee had been met by a squadron of British; a lively but unequal battle had followed in which the German ships had been defeated and sunk.

When I heard this I looked at Hoffmann who was sitting across the table. His face was pale and his eyes dreamy. After supper I took him aside to discuss the connection between his dream and the actual battle.

"Don't talk of it," he said in a whisper. "I want to forget it."

If I am not mistaken he never mentioned the coincidence again.

For the next few days we continued coaling and taking on provisions whenever the weather permitted. The sea, however, was rough. The *Bellevue* rubbed and bumped into our port so vehemently that our side sprung heavy leaks and streams of water poured into our bunkers. But as our supply of coal was dangerously low, we had to continue coaling at all costs.

When the sea became so turbulent that coaling would have been positively dangerous, we did not take the *Bellevue* alongside, but kept our men busy caulking the seams in our side, while our engines pumped out the bunkers, in one of which the water already stood two metres high. As military drill also was interspersed with other duties, the men were kept busy from morning till night.

In time to break this busy round of work, on Friday afternoon at five o'clock the alarm sounded "Clear for action!" A steamer had been sighted. The men took their stations with alacrity, thinking that sport was at hand.

The sighted ship, however, proved to be the German steamer *Otavi* of Hamburg, for which Commander Thierfelder had been waiting some days. The *Otavi*, which now took her position on our port, had been ten days on her way from Pernambuco to bring us provisions and fresh water and to take ashore the crews of the *Anne de Bretagne,* the *Mont Agel,* and the *Bellevue.* During the following ten days that she remained with us she stayed constantly on the port side of the *Kronprinz* so as not to be seen by our prisoners of war whose windows all looked to starboard.

The Sunday following was to some extent a disappointment to our men who were accustomed to having the Sabbath off after 11 A. M. This Sunday, however, was so fine a day, with so favourable a sea, that Commander Thierfelder took the *Bellevue* alongside and made the men coal all day. To encourage them, however, he had the war news which the *Otavi* brought read aloud, and the men showed their appreciation by working diligently, taking aboard a larger quantity of coal than had been expected.

I said that the *Bellevue* had on board a large cellar of assorted wines and whiskies. Now, sailors, as all men

A brisk race gave the KRONPRINZ *the* MONT AGEL *and her meagre cargo: one pig, one ox, six sheep, and a few provisions. The upper picture shows the* KRON-PRINZ *actually ramming the prize.*

know, have good noses for whisky, and our men were not long in finding means to poach upon the *Bellevue's* supply. While coaling they found time to steal bottles of the liquor, sometimes even shoving them into the coal sacks and thus sending them to their friends on deck. But, as drunkenness on duty is a court-martial offence, of which the men were repeatedly reminded by the commander, the thirsty seamen saved their stolen supplies until they came off duty, when they went below decks, hid themselves, and "fired up." Old Smuggler and Black Horse were their favourites, as we could tell by the empty bottles found in corners. Many more empty flasks must have been thrown overboard, as the count of the number of cases taken on board added to the number of empty bottles found did not tally with that shown in the ship's papers.

It has been said that "a sailor has a weak head and a strong stomach." But our men must have had pretty strong heads also to guzzle on the sly without showing the effects. It may be that I am doing the men an injustice; perhaps only a few of them took nips now and then. This much is certain: on the whole cruise I do not remember seeing one man drunk. If a case occurred the man or his friends certainly used some excellent strategy to keep the fact from the officers. Discipline aboard a German man-o'-war is so strict that a summary example would have been made of the first offender caught.

In addition to the whisky which so much delighted the crew, the *Bellevue* also carried some bicycles and two automobiles with numerous extra parts. These vehicles were now to afford much amusement to our men. An automobile engine was at once taken out of one of the automobiles and built into a lifeboat to convert the craft into a launch. The building in of the engine was quickly accomplished by our machinists who went about the work with the zeal of boys making a toy, while our coppersmiths fashioned a neat and shiny propeller.

When the engine had been installed the question of fuel arose, for the *Kronprinz* had no gasoline on board. This question, to be sure, had been broached before work on the engine began, but the general hope had been that we might soon obtain some gasoline from a captured prize. The men were anxious to try the launch without delay. They wanted to play with their toy.

A bright idea now occurred to one of them: he suggested using whisky in place of gasoline. The happy notion was acted on in a trice; the gasoline tank was partly filled with the cherry-coloured liquid from numerous bottles, the launch lowered into the sea, and a trial made. The engine, however, refused to work well. On being urged it made a few revolutions, exploding with a soggy sound, and then stopped completely. A sorry waste of good whisky. So after trying all afternoon to make the engine run on whisky the men finally gave the task up as immoral.

"You can make a man work on alcohol," they jocularly remarked, "but the guts of an engine prefer gas."

On the same afternoon that the trial of the launch was

made, some of the men who were off duty, not knowing that the launch was going to prove a failure, got the commander's permission to take the second automobile on the starboard promenade deck in the hope of running the vehicle for pleasure. After pumping up the tires and filling the tank with whisky a trial was made. The automobile, however, also refused to run on whisky.

At this the sailors were much disappointed and they went over to the men at the launch, who were now having a similar experience, to tell them their labours were for nothing. The self-starter on the automobile, charged by the ship's dynamos, had given them the advantage of trying out the engine thoroughly in a short time. Soon, true to their jolly spirit, they returned to their toy and began amusing themselves by pushing the automobile up and down. A dozen lusty fellows crowded into the car like a party off for a picnic, while a team of another dozen got behind and pushed. The "honk! honk!" of the horn above the cheering of the men out there in the middle of the ocean was ludicrous beyond conception.

When the vehicle reached one end of the deck, the pushing team ran around to the front and pushed the automobile back again. Then it was their turn to climb in and to be pushed. A very childish sport, to be sure. But you must remember that men are only grown-up boys, and these men had been out of sight of the pleasures of land for more than a third of a year.

It should be added that later on when gasoline became

accessible both automobile and launch worked to perfection, in some measure compensating the mechanics who had put them together.

I must not forget to mention that the men also busied themselves with still another pastime as a result of the capture of the *Bellevue*. Of the coloured wool and fine white linen which were found in the cargo of this ship they made beautiful table centrepieces. Many of our men were excellent needleworkers, having learned the art on previous voyages while trying to pass their idle time. These centrepieces were intended for ultimate sale, but I am afraid that few were disposed of in this manner, as most of the treasures were given to the lady prisoners from ships we soon afterward captured. These feminine sirens well knew how to beg for the needlework, and a stupid fellow who has not seen a woman for a long time can easily be wheedled out of his possessions.

While these diversions were taking place the serious business of the ship was of course not neglected. For some days we took the *Bellevue* and the *Otavi* by turns on our port, alternately coaling from the one and taking on fresh water, provisions, wine, champagne, cigars, cigarettes, and clothing from the other. On Sunday at 6 A. M. we sighted a sail, but were too busy to give chase as we wanted to finish unloading the *Bellevue* that morning and send her to the bottom. There still remained some whisky and cognac, but these were soon brought aboard. Then all hands were ordered to leave the steamer, save a few who remained to lash down the lifeboats together with whatever else could float about and reveal the location of the destruction.

While this was being done the *Bellevue* was set adrift and the *Kronprinz* backed away. Then, when all were ready, the men aboard the doomed vessel opened the seacocks and hastened over the side into their waiting boat.

For once we were not in a great hurry to see a steamer settle and sink as a result of opening her seacocks. We felt ourselves secure from danger. A cable's length off to port the *Otavi* was waiting for us to finish unloading her. So we brought this vessel alongside and began taking on provisions, fresh water, beer, cigars, cigarettes, and clothing while waiting for the *Bellevue* to sink.

I went to the rail many times to photograph and watch the doomed ship. At about three thirty I could see her begin to list to port. Then at four she suddenly leaned farther over, rolled like a sea lion, and gracefully slid into the sea. All in a moment it seemed as if the splendid steamer of a minute before had never existed.

The *Bellevue* thus off our hands, we now hastened our provisioning from the *Otavi*. In return for the latter's plenteous bounty we gave the ship a small supply of much-needed coal. At the same time we sent aboard her all our prisoners of war who were glad of a change which gave them hope of soon reaching port.

This transfer of prisoners was quite picturesque. Most of the men were in cheerful mood; they walked with light step, and deporting themselves in a where-do-we-go-from-here spirit. When they got aboard the *Otavi* they paused along the rail to look us over, as most of them were curious to see once more the ship which had so long carried them without allowing them a glimpse of her exterior. At 9:30 P. M. the little ship left our side to wait at a short distance before leaving next day.

The reason for this delay became apparent the first thing in the morning. It happened that three members of the *Otavi's* crew and one of her passengers had on the day before each lost some baggage overboard when a hoisting cable which was transferring the packages broke, precipitating the bundles into the sea. These men were now rowed over to us by some of our crew to receive indemnity. After giving a brief description of his loss the first was awarded fifty shillings; the next two each received 120 shillings; but the fourth, the passenger, a fat, squat man with greenish eyes and a red nose, demanded too high a price. He had lost a fur-lined coat, he said, alone worth fifty pounds, and a suit worth fifteen pounds. Our purser, suspecting fraud, offered the man 120 shillings, the same amount he had offered the two sailors preceding. But the man, a civilian, unused to the politeness with which men in service speak to officers, was obdurate and even offensive.

"You call yourselves honest," he said haughtily. "Prove it! My suit and coat were worth sixty-five pounds and I want all or none. I'll put in a complaint as soon as I reach port."

"Can you prove the value of your coat?" he was asked.

"Yes, I can refer you to the house that sold it."

This seemed distant proof. Meanwhile, his three companions kept shaking their heads behind the man's back, as if to say: "Don't believe him. He's lying."

The officers in charge had these men taken aside and questioned.

"He's the biggest liar on the ship," they declared. "You can't believe a word he says. Besides, we don't believe he had a suit of clothes in the bundle that went overboard. He could just as well have had blankets in that bundle."

The matter was finally settled by giving the man a suit of clothes and a pair of shoes with the advice to put in his additional claim with the proofs after the war.

The argument at an end, the four men were rowed back to the *Otavi* and our boat returned, when with cheers and waving of hands on the part of departing passengers and crew, answered by cheers from our men, the *Otavi* steamed off for home, leaving us once more alone on the restless Atlantic. We waited at a standstill until the ship was out of sight, then picked up our speed to the east-southeast on the hunt for more prizes.

That was Monday, the twenty-first of December. At 5 P. M. the commander ordered all hands to assemble on the poop. When he arrived his face was serious. He began to speak in a calm and subdued voice. What he said we officers had known since the eighth of December. On that day, as mentioned, a squadron of five German cruisers had engaged eight British warships off the Falkland Islands. The *Scharnhorst, Gneisenau,* and *Leipzig* had been sunk; the *Nürnberg* had taken flight in a burning condition and perhaps foundered. Only the *Dresden* had escaped. The losses of the English had been unimportant.

This news sank into the hearts of our men. Many had friends aboard the sunken vessels whom they now would never see again. Also, a premonition of a like fate for themselves occurred to their minds. Hitherto the actions of the German ships had resulted in daring victory. This undoubted defeat only showed how helpless a ship is when met by an enemy with greater speed and guns of longer range. Our crew disbanded quietly, sober determination in their looks, and there was a kind of mourning quiet all over the ship the rest of that evening.

I found Hoffmann in his room that night writing a letter.

"I sent a letter home by the *Otavi,*" he said. "Now I'm writing one toward the time we meet another ship bound for the world of people. I wonder what the home folks think about us—whether we are alive or dead, wounded or sound, happy or sad?"

"You're quite anticlimacteric," I laughed.

"Well," he answered, "we're a good long way from home, that is sure, and the Lord knows how much nearer the bottom of the ocean than the roof over our hearths. But Christmas will be here in a few days and then for a good time. It may be our last."

Chapter XIV

A CHRISTMAS WITH SHARKS IN THE TROPICS

CHRISTMAS! We were on the high seas, at war, and in the tropics into the bargain, but Christmas— that is a time to make a man's heart leap no matter where he is or in what condition are the affairs of the world.

On the twenty-second the preparation of the ship began. From stem to stern the *Kronprinz Wilhelm* was given a thorough scouring, while painting was done wherever a spot needed it. The men worked with spirit, enthusiastic over the coming events.

We would have Christmas trees, too, even though we were a hundred miles from the nearest forest. The men were already busy below decks fashioning pine-tree trunks of sticks into which they bored holes for holding branches —also sticks—with needles of painted broom straws wired to them. These trees were marvellously lifelike. It is truly astonishing what patience achieved in creating the minutest resemblance to life. Even pine cones were carved to such perfection that it took close scrutiny to detect the imitation.

The trees were placed in different parts of the ship,

for, as the grand saloon was now our reserve bunker, there was no one hall large enough for all, and the crew had to celebrate by divisions.

The different rooms were draped with division banners, hung with green tissue paper, and painted with woodland scenery, while coloured electric lights were strung upon the trees with the ornaments and gifts.

The ornaments consisted of chains of coloured paper, and of an endless variety of trinkets, not to mention twisted candles, brought by the *Prussia,* while spangles of glass glittered in the coloured light. The whole was as yulelike as man could conceive.

The celebration was scheduled for Thursday, the evening of the twenty-fourth. I shall never forget the anxiety the men felt lest something happen which would put an end to the celebration. On the day preceding, for instance, we sighted a steamship and everyone thought: "If this is a prize we may have to work all Christmas."

The ship, however, was a Dutchman and was allowed to proceed. On Thursday, Christmas Eve, at four o'clock, a second ship was sighted, but this also proved to be a neutral, a Spaniard, and was not stopped. The men, once more breathing freely and hoping they had been interrupted for the last time, made ready for the celebration. This getting ready included taking the regular bath, brushing up the uniform, and getting a haircut.

The barber shop was a large room on the starboard side of the ship opening on the promenade deck just above the firemen's deck—a converted first-class cabin. Its only furniture was a plush sofa and a chair, both fastened to a linoleum-covered floor. In this room was always to be found a goodly company of seamen who had excellent reasons for being attracted thither. In the first place the barber himself, a short Berliner with square ears and a turned-up nose, was an extremely clever fellow. Speaking rapidly and with a Berliner accent, he could keep the men amused, telling them the drollest stories for the fiftieth time, yet never tiring them or failing to delight. Often he would entertain by discussing the ruses by which a barber persuades a man to have his hair cut or shampooed or singed against his will. Being a Berliner, he had the self-assurance characteristic of his city—believed, in short, that he could outwit any man, and was ready to prove it.

His wit showed itself in another way, which was the second reason for the popularity of his shop. For he had covered every square inch of the walls of his room with the pictures of naked women clipped from the London *Police Gazette*. These pictures stared a man in the face every way he looked and were the important study of the barber's clients. There was never a lack of company in the barber shop so long as the hair cutter was there and the lights were turned on.

The barber himself, a perfectly human chap, was a member of my own division; and as it was my duty to defend my men against accusations I was often hard put to find excuses for the trouble into which the fellow got himself by his overnimble wit.

Sometimes, for instance, he would sell his perfumes at extortionate prices, and, when questioned, frankly admitt that he was profiteering. But what of it? Had he not a right to sell at whatever figure he liked? The men did not have to buy. If they wanted the cologne let them pay his price. And when one listened to the man talk in this strain for a few minutes one was at a loss what to answer. He was so nimble in his speech the injured customer almost felt repaid in hearing the flow of oratory which the question caused.

There was only one man aboard ship whom the barber could not impose on, and this man had the Berliner at his mercy. This was none other than our ex-comedian Scholke. Scholke and the barber got on famously. When the comedian was present the two engaged in repartee which would set the men laughing until they rolled off the sofa and burst out of the door to prevent rupturing their sides. Whenever a great noise was heard in the direction of the barber shop the men would prick their ears with the remark: "Scholke's in there again."

On this afternoon before Christmas the shop was unusually crowded; the Berliner was working so fast he hardly had time to say more than "What kind?" "How short?" and "Next!"

But toward four o'clock, when business was at its height, the shop was suddenly almost emptied by news which took the men out on the run. Not even the sounding of "Clear for action!" could have cleared the premises so quickly. The dog Nelka, the ship's mascot, presented to the *Kronprinz* by the officers and men of the *Walhalla,* had given birth to three puppies.

Everyone wanted to see the puppies. There was a great gathering on the firemen's deck where Nelka's kennel was kept, and in the general excitement Christmas was forgotten until one man sang out:

"Three puppies—a Christmas present from Nelka to the *Kronprinz!*"

The proud mother seemed to share the general enthusiasm and let the men handle the puppies. She was panting a good bit and her tongue hung out on account of the heat, while she kept a wary eye lest any of her precious ones come to harm. The crew, on general principles, looked upon the Christmas gift as an omen of good.

Thus Christmas Eve arrived. At four-thirty everything was ready, all hands except a few were off duty, and the celebration began.

Punctually at five o'clock the men were assembled and a solemn invocation to the Deity was offered up. Then the crew feasted upon a banquet of stout fare, with pastries, wines, and delicacies taken from captured vessels, after which the men dispersed to the various rooms where the celebrations were to take place.

The crew had invited the officers to attend their celebrations. Shortly after six o'clock a deputation waited on us to request our attendance, and at six-ten we began making the rounds, first separating into five parties, each of which was to visit a different division and then gradually go around to the others in the course of the evening.

I entered the hall of the first division just as the men were going into the room. It was an inspiration to be present. Inside the room all lights were out save those on the beautiful yule tree. As the men filed in their orchestra began playing "O Tannenbaum," the men picking up the tender tune, some singing, some whistling, some humming. Then all gathered in a semicircle, joined hands, and finished the last stanza of the song together, beating time by regularly raising and lowering their interlocked hands. Then silence fell, and the oldest of their number advanced in front of the glittering tree, knelt, bowed his head, and in low tones spoke a benediction.

I was now called on to make a speech. I spoke a few words, trying to be brief, well knowing that the men were anxious to see their presents. After this I assisted the rest of the officers in taking presents from the tree, while one of us called out the names of the recipients. These promptly came forward, their faces glowing, and claimed the gifts.

Every man received several presents—rich ones under the circumstances. The floor was strewn with heaps of paper wrappers, tissue-paper linings, and so forth. As a gift from the ship, each man received fifty cigarettes, ten cigars, two shirts, some soap, some Christmas cakes, some loose tobacco, and a few other odds and ends. In addition, most of the men were given presents by their personal friends.

We officers received splendid gifts from each division as a whole, but the best present of all was the good will which the men showed toward us. We felt that no man owed us a grudge—a comfortable feeling to a naval officer on a long cruise, I can assure you.

I visited each of the divisions in turn, everywhere finding the genial spirit of good will to men beaming on all countenances. This night was the one night of the year when the men permitted themselves to become familiar with us. It was: "Count, have a cigar!"—"Lieutenant, take a cake, please."—"Some candy, Count!"—"A glass of wine, Count!"—and so on.

That night at ten o'clock a sailing vessel came near us on our port side, but Commander Thierfelder refused to break the Christmas festivities to halt her. At two in the morning a steamer was sighted, but was likewise passed by. Again at four in the morning a second steamer came within view and was similarly ignored. The sacred festivity of Christmas, 1914, passed without a hostile stroke, though I am sure Commander Thierfelder was sorely tempted by the steamers.

When the morning of the twenty-fifth dawned all men were up and at work despite the night's revelry. By ten o'clock the ship had been policed and all hands were given a holiday. Shortly after 10 A. M. a general raffle of 454 presents was made among the 454 men on our ship, each man receiving one. At noon these presents were supplemented with a bottle of beer. To crown all the *Weihnachts-zeitung,* or Christmas newspaper, appeared with its columns of absurd news, droll jokes, and fraudulent advertisements. All hands at once forgot themselves in the reading of the four-page sheet, as happy as if they had a treasure.

At 2:45 P. M. it began to look like work again. A sailing vessel appeared upon the horizon bearing from the south, and the *Kronprinz Wilhelm,* sounding "Clear for action!" made toward her. But she proved to be the *Celtic Queen,* a Norwegian, so we let her proceed. As we steamed by her she signalled, asking for her bearings. But since to give these would have disclosed our own position we merely signalled: "Merry Christmas!" and steamed on. The *Celtic Queen* took a northwesterly course and soon disappeared over the horizon, evidently bound for home. As she disappeared the band began playing for us, and Christmas ended as happily as it had begun.

Christmas was thus a merry time aboard the *Kronprinz,* but the days that immediately followed were not so happy. On the morning of the twenty-sixth a leak was discovered in the port propeller-shaft well, and an investigation disclosed that the steel sides of the well had been fractured, causing a dangerous leak.

This was dismaying news. To mend the fractured well on the high seas was an impossibility, while if the crack extended itself the propeller would be crippled. The *Kronprinz* could of course continue with only one propeller, but at less than half speed. The ship, in consequence, would be at the mercy of the enemy. This news, at first kept secret, soon spread to the crew, putting a damper on the post-Christmas cheer.

This depression was soon to pass, however. On Monday the twenty-eighth at 5 P. M., after we had spent the day at hard military drill, a steamer came in sight. "Clear for action!" sounded and all hands sped to station with a feeling that real action was a relief.

Putting on all speed, though with a misgiving lest the port propeller well come to grief, we reached the enemy at six o'clock. The ship proved to be the one-funnelled steamer *Hemisphere* of Liverpool, a vessel of 3,486 gross tons, on her way from Hull, England, to La Plata.

The *Hemisphere* was an old, low-lying steamer, painted black save for her white cabin and lifeboats, her gray deck, and a light band around her funnel. Below the water line she was the usual red. In her hold she carried four thousand five hundred tons of cargo coal in addition to one thousand six hundred tons in her bunkers. Of provisions she had almost none at all; in fact, she had hardly enough to feed her crew. When asked why he was so short of provisions, the captain explained that prices in England were so high he was forced to calculate to a pound the minimum amount of provisions necessary for the trip, and that when he submitted this budget some articles were deducted from it as not absolutely necessary. He intimated that he had grumbled at the time about the stinginess of his company, but was glad now because the extra provisions would only have fallen to us, the enemy.

The *Hemisphere* had used no wireless when we first gave chase, which somewhat puzzled us, but we now learned that the vessel bore no wireless; in fact, she was so old and leaked so badly that her company did not think her worth equipping with a wireless set.

Her crew, which now came aboard the *Kronprinz* as prisoners of war, deported themselves discreetly, gave no trouble while being searched, and soon looked at home in their second-class quarters. A division of our men at once rowed over to the prize to man the ship and get all ready. Soon afterward, part of a second division also was dispatched to the *Hemisphere* to put coal into sacks and help make all ready for unloading. By Wednesday, the thirtieth, everything was in readiness. The *Hemisphere* was brought round on our port, coaling promptly began, and by nightfall we had taken aboard 542 tons.

Meanwhile, the weather had become splendid and as the early morning of the thirtieth advanced our men noticed many man-eating sharks swimming about our ship. Now, fishing for sharks is one of the sailor's keenest sports. This outlaw of the sea, which bites a man in two or mangles him as mercilessly as an engine, arouses in the seaman a savage spite. Unlike the harmless fish which is caught for food, the man-eating shark appears to the mariner as a natural enemy, his legitimate prey, an evil power of the deep, ordained to destroy and to be destroyed.

Once, off the coast of Mexico, I saw a sailor's foot bitten off as his legs dangled in the water, where he was sitting on a plank painting the ship's side. The man was hurried ashore, but before medical aid reached him he had died of loss of blood. The picture of surprise and anguish on that man's face as the shark struck will stay with me for life. Only mention shark to a sailor and you will see his eye glint and his fist clench.

On this particular thirtieth of December, 1914, as coaling from the *Hemisphere* progressed, those of our men who happened to be off duty dug their sharking tackle out of the ship's hold and began the sport.

Under ordinary conditions, the sport of catching sharks is a fascinating one, not without its danger. A hook of half-inch steel some nine inches in semicircumference with a shank about two feet long is forged. To it is fastened about a yard of heavy chain, and to the chain a tough hempen cable. As the shark may weigh from a few pounds to as high as several hundred pounds, and the single strength of a man would be powerless against its savage efforts when once the hook is tearing its jaws, the cable is passed through a pulley lashed to a davit, and a number of men stand ready to pull together when the struggle begins.

A few pounds of pork are now lashed about the sharp point of the hook, the men stand back, one of them swings the bait around his head by the end of the chain, and with the cable coiling behind it, off it shoots into the sea where the cynical man-eaters are alert for prey.

Now, a hundred eagle eyes search the blue water. Soon a glittering flash appears a dozen yards from the bait, the water parts, and up cuts the triangular, steel-like, dorsal fin of a full-sized man-eater.

Now, the mouth of the great white shark is so far back on the under side of its head and curves in such a backward manner that the creature cannot bite a floating object unless it first turns completely over. As the huge fish gets within a few yards of the bait its body describes a lateral curve, the perpendicular fin which till now has alone been visible above the surface splashes under on the right side of the body, and the glistening white belly scintillates against the sky as the saw-ridged jaws open for the bait.

At this instant the men on board spring to life. One swift pull on the cable jerks the point of the hook fast into the shark's mouth. The next instant the men are hauling in on the cable. If the prize is particularly large and of unusual strength other seamen who have been watching the sport run up and help to haul it from the water.

When the body, splashing furiously, leaves the sea it swings against the ship, and the flapping, lashing, writhing beast tattoos savagely against the steel plates of the vessel. The nose of the fighting monster is drawn up to the very pulley; two seamen, watching their chance, warily pass a cable around its tail, and, all hands pulling together, the giant prize is hauled on deck, where it flays about in blind fury.

Sometimes, instead of a hook, a mere chain with bait is thrown overboard and the sailors lay by on deck ready with rifles. A shark's back and sides are practically bullet-proof, but when the monster turns over to swallow its prey its soft white belly makes an excellent target. The men shoot into the white, and watch with grim satisfaction the stream of blood which stains the water behind the rapidly careering body.

When properly treated a shark's skin can be made into souvenirs. Back of the head, a shark bears a pouch of fat which when rightly cooked and liquefied makes the purest kind of oil for lubricating watches and delicate instruments. The jaw and head bones are cleaned and sold to dealers in curios. But best of all, the sturdy backbone can be made into an excellent cane. The separate verte-bræ, after being well cleaned, are strung like beads upon a piece of steel wire which runs lengthwise through the empty channel left by the removal of the spinal cord. Pieces of coloured wood are then inserted in the regular holes on the side of the bones. The whole is finally sand-papered and varnished. These canes are much esteemed and sell at high prices. Our ship acquired quite a stock of them.

The men who had begun the sport that morning were soon joined by others. Hearing the shouts that went up as the lusty fishermen became more exhilarated with the game, those of the crew who were enjoying a nap below decks during their off shift came up and likewise took part in the sport. The biting and catching were exceptionally rapid. The sea seemed fairly to swarm with the monsters. Had a man fallen overboard that day there would have been nothing left of him a minute later.

By twelve o'clock the sport had become so exciting that it was only with effort that the men who were coaling could refrain from witnessing the fun. All the larger sharks caught were killed and kept on deck until their bones and oil could be removed. The whole firemen's deck was soon piled high with them. By three in the afternoon I counted fifty man-eaters—some of them monsters ten feet long.

For the next two days there was a great cutting up of shark carcasses. When the valuable bones and fat had been removed the rest of the shark was thrown overboard, for the meat of this fish is not edible, and even if it were the sailor's resentment against this mortal enemy would prevent him from touching it.

Inspired by the excitement of this unprecedented shark catch, next day, Thursday, the last day of the year 1914, our men set a coaling record, 713 tons being brought aboard on that day. This was a triumphant close to the year marked by so much surprise, anguish, and toil.

That night, the night all men stay up to see the new year in, Hoffmann proposed that a company of us officers gather in the Wiener Kaffee and have a good time. Nine o'clock was set for the gathering to which all of our little clique who were off duty promised to come.

Hoffmann and I had just finished an exciting game of chess which had lasted since seven, when punctually at nine o'clock the first man, Lieutenant Emil Biermann, came yodling in. Biermann was a tall fellow, fully six feet six. We called him *Der lange Emil*—The long Emil—a man as fastidious in his dress and general habits as a teacher at the Naval Academy. He slapped Hoffmann on the shoulder, bowed to me with an habitual "Count Von!" and launched into a tirade about the "dirty coaling business."

After a few minutes, Lieutenant Forstreuter silently stepped in. Forstreuter, as honest a man as God ever made, had of late been quite downcast. His home was in East Prussia—Tilsit on the Memel, to be exact. His people had a beautiful estate there where I had hoped, if all went well, to spend some delightful vacations. But only a few months back the man had received the terrible news that East Prussia had been overrun by the Russians, his birth town destroyed, his beautiful home burned to the ground, and his estate laid waste with fire and ax. Where his parents and sisters were or what their fate, he had no knowledge. In the end, fate was perhaps kind to him, for he lost his life on the ill-starred *Eclipse* before he had time to learn the full story of the misfortunes of his family.

Next came in Lieutenant Fix and Doctor Kaspar, the two most sedate of our company, followed by Lieutenant

Rüdebusch, a gentleman and a good fellow. We seven made up the party that night, ever memorable to those of us who are still alive.

I say "still alive," for of these seven, four, Lieutenants Rüdebusch, Forstreuter, Biermann, and Hoffmann, all went down on the luckless *Eclipse*.

Rüdebusch now set the victrola going and the machine churned out our old stand-by—"O Isabella." That piece was as popular on the *Kronprinz Wilhelm* as "K-K-K-Katy" was in the American army. This night no sooner did the graphophone start playing it than some seamen on the promenade deck picked up the tune, and "O Isabella" was relayed down into the hold, where those of the men not on duty had decorated their rooms and were also celebrating.

After a game of cards, Hoffmann proposed that each man tell a story. The *Decameron* and the *Arabian Nights* at once came to my mind, making me welcome the suggestion, and as the rest were equally romantically inclined, the motion was carried.

As someone had to begin, I told the story of my great-grandfather's adventure at the battle of Vienna against the Turks in 1683. In proof of the story I showed my signet ring, which bore the family coat of arms, bestowed upon my ancestor for his part in that battle.

Hoffmann told the next story—a love story in which he figured as protagonist and the girl as antagonist.

"In proof," he ended with a suggestive glance at the

The HEMISPHERE, *a post-Christmas prize.*

ceiling above my head, "in proof of the truth of this story, witness that I wear no ring on my finger, my ring with the family coat of arms having been tossed into the deep well that tragic night, as I have just recounted."

Grave Fix now began a solemn tale of the first mate aboard the *Bellevue*, from which, however, he shortly broke off, saying that he had better not tell it as it was too personal. Besides, he always spoiled a tale. We tried to coax him but with no success, and he passed around cigars as a forfeit.

Doctor Kaspar then told some gruesome jokes of the dissecting room, and Rüdebusch whistled a few Oriental tunes in lieu of a story. Biermann told some more jokes, and Forstreuter related the details of a great rat-catching he had witnessed as a child in the stables on his estate, when all his servants and their relatives had come from far and near on a day to make general and united war upon the pests.

If the evening had stopped then, we should have counted it most successful. All were in good humour, everyone feeling as Old-Yearly-and-about-to-become-New-Yearly as good cheer and wine could make us, when suddenly Fix decided that he would tell us his story anyway. He wanted to get it off his mind.

This sounded as ominous as it proved in the end to be. In his slow, grave, composed voice, slightly sad on this evening, he told us a story which the captured first mate of the *Bellevue* had told him.

On a previous voyage with another ship on which he was second mate, his senior, the first mate, was under suspicion of being a German spy, and was consequently closely watched, though the man himself was not aware of it. On the first day out from Liverpool the ship was suddenly brought to a stop by an inquiry as to one of the crank bearings of its engine, which for some mysterious reason had become overheated and was ground up. It was at once suspected that someone had dropped emery into the lubrication of the bearing to cripple the engine and stop the ship. For at this time the submarine danger was growing daily and a ship at a standstill is a good target for a torpedo.

Now, the captain of the ship was a man of extraordinary strength and bulldog ferocity. Enraged to discover treachery aboard his ship and thinking the first mate guilty, he held an informal and summary court-martial. The second mate had nothing incriminating to report, nor had the engineers, with the exception of the chief engineer who said he had seen the first mate in the engine room some time prior to the accident.

The first mate admitted having been in the engine room, but only to borrow some tobacco from the chief engineer; he protested his innocence. But the captain had already jumped to his conclusion. Hot words passed and the first mate was ordered to keep to his room.

That night was a stormy one. At about eleven o'clock,

when the ship which had been stopped twelve hours by the accident was again in motion, the captain went to the first mate's room, ordered him out, and walked with him to the pitch dark poop. Five minutes later he rushed back, alone, and signalled to the engineer: "Full speed astern!" The first mate, he said, had jumped overboard.

Of course a search at night in such a sea was a mere pretense. After a brief stop the acetylene buoy which the captain had thrown overboard was fished up, and the ship again got under way. When he reached port the captain sent in his report that the first mate, caught in a treasonable act, had committed suicide.

For prudential reasons the second mate kept his counsel, but he had noted on the night of the crime that when the captain left him at the wheel to go aft with the first mate his coat was buttoned, but when he came back and shouted that the first mate was overboard three buttons were missing from his coat and a bleeding scratch ran diagonally across his throat.

"And worst of all," the mate told Fix, "when we started back on our homeward trip we had not got twenty-four hours out of Hoboken when the same accident happened to the same bearing of the engine, delaying us for almost the same length of time—and this time I was the first mate."

Fix stopped here. We plied him with questions to learn what came of the matter. Was the captain ever exposed? What was the matter with the bearing? What was the name of the mate? But Fix answered that the mate did not seem to want to mention names, as the captain might some day "get him."

The angry feeling of my fellow officers, stirred by this tale of cold-blooded murder, now broke forth in eloquent profanity directed at the fiendish captain, when suddenly the great, deep-toned whistle of our ship gave a long, deafening New Year hoot.

Instinctively every man was on his feet.

"*Prost Neujahr!*" we shouted all at the same time, and grasping hands we shook them with all our might.

Nineteen hundred and fifteen was here. Hail to her birth! The *Kronprinz Wilhelm* had steamed into a new year.

Chapter XV

THE "POTARO," THE "HIGHLAND BRAE," AND THE "WILFRED M." GIVE THE "KRONPRINZ" ACTION

WITH the coming of the new year events seemed to move more rapidly. From intercepted wireless messages we knew that the British, alarmed at the heavy toll of ships we were taking, were making redoubled efforts to cut us off. About eighty detached war vessels were on the hunt for commerce raiders on the Atlantic, the *Kronprinz Wilhelm* being especially sought. Each day Brinkmann told us of some new development in the chase, warned us of danger, and acted generally as the eye of the ship.

Meanwhile, the well of our broken propeller shaft was giving us increasing concern. It seemed that as the danger from pursuit grew the disabilities of the ship also increased. We began to go to bed with the feeling that perhaps before morning the ship would be at a standstill as a result of an accident to propellers or engine. Despite constant repair the *Kronprinz* seemed gradually sinking into worse condition. Boiler tubes blew out frequently, engine trouble occurred more often than before, and the port side of the ship itself, despite constant caulking, leaked more every day.

The first day of the new year was spent coaling, 652 tons being that day's record. Next day we took aboard 584 tons, and on Sunday forenoon 209.5 tons. Then a holiday was declared. At three o'clock the band played on the promenade deck, after which the commander talked to the men on the forward deck concerning the achievements during the five months the ship had cruised about the Atlantic.

The *Kronprinz Wilhelm,* leaving Hoboken on the night of August 3, 1914, had up to January 1, 1915, steamed more than 20,000 miles—five sixths the distance around the earth—and in doing so had burned more than twenty thousand tons of coal. Only one third of this fuel had been taken from German ships; the rest was confiscated from the enemy. About half of the food supply, also, had been furnished by enemy vessels. The *Kronprinz,* therefore, had been of relatively small expense to the Fatherland.

During the voyage, furthermore, certain curious facts had presented themselves. In the identical spot, for instance, in which we had captured the *Bellevue* and *Mont Agel* we had formerly taken the steamer *Indian Prince,* while we had captured the *Union* in the same place we had previously overtaken the *La Correntina.* All of the vessels, moreover, which had been sent out by the admiralty to coal and provision us had returned safely to their bases. In addition, we had crossed the equator five times. On the whole the voyage was a great success.

After this heartening summary of their five months' toil the crew dispersed to its various pleasures. I was watching the men disband when Hoffmann laid his hand on my shoulder.

"Niezy," he said, "let's go aft and shoot porpoises. I haven't used my revolver for an age."

We accordingly went to the poop rail, where we had hardly begun to look for porpoises when a second idea occurred to my friend.

"Niezy," he exclaimed with a glad ring in his voice, "did you ever notice the *Hemisphere's* anchors? Well, I haven't had any fun since Christmas. Let's throw the *Hemisphere's* anchors overboard. Fix is Officer of the Day. When he hears the noise he'll do a war dance."

This sounded like fun, so over to the *Hemisphere* we went. At the forecastle head we found the anchor chains neatly laid out. The anchors themselves were huge ten-ton patent ones, very valuable if we could have used them. The *Kronprinz,* however, had two fifteen-ton patent anchors, so that these of the *Hemisphere* would go down with the ship.

In all haste Hoffmann and I now went to work, fearing that Fix might catch us before we got the anchor loose. In a few minutes, however, the chain was clear. Then Hoffmann threw back the anchor clutch, when with a piercing screech the massive chain clattered outward, throwing up a cloud of sparks and rust dust as the ten-ton anchor plunged into the sea.

The water spurted up higher than the forecastle head. But Hoffmann and I did not stop to watch it. We got out of sight on the port side of the *Hemisphere's* cabin just as Fix's voice rang out from the bridge.

"What's the matter there?"

There was no answer. We could hardly hold our sides from bursting to think how Fix's always serious face must look at that instant.

At last a seaman on the *Kronprinz Wilhelm* sang out:

"Starboard anchor on the *Hemisphere* gone overboard, sir, and chain, too, sir."

Fix at once made an investigation, which we did not stay to witness.

That evening when we told him who had done the deed the good-natured fellow only smiled.

"I knew who it must be," he said. "A seaman would never dare, and any officers but you two would never think of such foolishness."

We asked Commander Thierfelder's permission to throw the other anchor overboard next day. As that anchor was also of no use to the *Kronprinz*, he readily granted the request. We forgot all about this anchor, however, until the day the vessel itself was sent to the bottom, when we were too busy for sport.

The next two days were spent in rapid coaling. On Wednesday morning, however, we sighted a ship. "Clear for action!" sounded, and the *Kronprinz* steered for the stranger. But the prize proved none other than the Ger-

man ship *Holger* of the Roland Line, Bremen, a freight
tramp without passenger accommodations. Commander
Thierfelder had been waiting for this ship some days. The
Holger took her position in our wake and followed us
back to the *Hemisphere*.

That afternoon, while we were manœuvring to bring
the *Hemisphere* on our port, the rudder chain of the prize
snapped. This caused not a little alarm as darkness was
about to set in and the ship would be helpless until the chain
should be repaired.

Our chief engineer immediately went over to the vessel,
set his men swiftly to work, and in the short space of an
hour had the rudder chain connected and working.

That evening I made an unimportant but interesting discovery on board the *Hemisphere*. Hoffmann and I were
going over the ship to note whether the men might not
have overlooked something of value, when it occurred to
me to read the ship's bells. Every ship carries at least two
bells, a small one at the bridge and a larger one at the
foremast, both stamped with the name of the ship. It was
the practice of the *Kronprinz Wilhelm* to take off the bells
of captured vessels, but as we would need the bells of the
Hemisphere until the ship should be sent to the bottom, her
gong was still in place.

I now discovered that the gong which had doubtless
been with the ship since her launching bore a different
name from that of the vessel, while the bell at the forecastle head, a relatively new one, was stamped with the

name *Hemisphere*. To a seaman this meant that the *Hemisphere* had lately been rechristened, being in reality the former *Trade Wind*. This discovery quite elated Hoffmann and me.

It will be hard to realize how busy the *Kronprinz Wilhelm* from now on became. We thought we had been hard worked before, but now the drudgery seemed to double. During the next two weeks, in fact, except on Sundays, we had hardly a pause.

Coaling from the *Hemisphere* proceeded with utmost rapidity, the work being rendered the more difficult by the bad condition of the prize's hull. As the coaling proceeded the leaks in the ancient hold of the ship increased to menacing proportions. The prize seemed a veritable sieve, the water spurting in in regular spouts through seams and rivet holes. To increase this leakage, we inadvertently bumped and rubbed against the prize repeatedly, damaging her sides still more. To offset the leaking, the pumps of the *Hemisphere* were kept going constantly, but despite this the intake was so great that we were in constant fear lest she founder at our side.

By 4 P. M. on Thursday we successfully brought the coaling to an end, and the hold of the *Hemisphere* was empty. All men were then ordered over her side and the opening of her seacocks began. Despite the leaky condition of the ship, this was the work of only a few minutes. Then as the men ran out on deck and scrambled up our swaying ladders the *Kronprinz* let go and backed away.

At a short but safe distance we watched the steamer gradually settle. Yet, despite our forecastings, the sinking proved too slow. At three-thirty next morning the prize was still afloat, though her decks were awash and her end near. At four as the darkness of night was just beginning to merge into the gray of dawn, our lookout saw the old prize tilt slightly head foremost, her bow going under and her stern slightly rising. Then without a sound the *Hemisphere* slid under the surface.

The *Hemisphere* sunk, Commander Thierfelder turned his attention to refitting the *Holger* to accommodate our prisoners of war, all of whom were to be carried to land by this vessel. Cabin equipment was hoisted over to the *Holger*, a crew of mechanics and carpenters fitting it in place, and large quantities of provisions and tons of fresh water were stored in the vessel's hold. Meanwhile, those of our crew who remained on our decks were kept busy cleaning ship, painting, and repairing. When evening came, five cigars, a bottle of beer, and a glass of wine rewarded the efforts of each man. On Sunday everybody had a holiday after 10 A. M.

At twelve-thirty, however, all hands were called to station by the sound of the alarm. A ship bearing to the southwest lay on the horizon.

The *Kronprinz* at once put on eighteen miles speed, steering directly upon the stranger. As soon as the latter noted our action, she turned to starboard and steered away at full speed. We increased our own and a race set in. The stranger saw us gaining, began to veer more to starboard, saw that this would avail her nothing, again turned to port, and took a racing course parallel to our own.

Meanwhile, the fleeing vessel was frantically using her wireless, calling for help. She carried a powerful Marconi outfit which could be heard for 500 miles. Lieutenant Brinkmann, ready for this action, at once sparked in between, while one of his aides did the same with the set captured from the *La Correntina.*

We were sure of our prey. Slowly we gained upon the prize, coming within range at 1 : 30 P. M. As the steamer refused either to stop or to show her flag, we now fired a blank warning shot. Immediately the Blue Jack was run up, which signified that the ship's commander was a member of the British Naval Reserve. The steamer then came to a stop and awaited orders.

Two officers with our prize crew now rowed over to the vessel and discovered her to be the British steamer *Potaro* of Belfast, on her way from Liverpool to Montevideo, sailing in ballast.

Developments now become interesting. In the first place, the officers and crew of the *Potaro* were from first to last a very disagreeable set, irritating our men by their overbearing manner. All the officers proved to be members of the British Naval Reserve, haughty, inconsiderate, insolent, and the crew seemed to have absorbed this spirit to the uttermost, doing just as their officers did. The "Lime-juicers," as our men called them, offered querulous objections to everything, found fault with everything, and were even stupid enough to take us for fools.

This self-assurance showed itself in the very first action of the captain. When the man was brought to our deck, he made what he thought a plausible proposition to Commander Thierfelder.

"I am bound for Buenos Aires," he said, "to get a cargo of refrigerated meat. If you let me proceed, I'll take on this meat and set out again for home. We can agree upon a rendezvous. I'll then meet you, and after you have stocked up on my meat cargo you can send my ship to the bottom."

This proposition was too silly to be true. Commander Thierfelder asked the man what he expected to gain by such treachery to his country. The man did not have the ingenuity to invent a plausible excuse. He had simply taken our commander for a stupid German "Michael" who, of course, could be outwitted by any Englishman.

Commander Thierfelder politely laughed the proposition down, said something about "a bird in the hand," and told the man that he and his crew were prisoners of war, would be treated as such, and would most probably soon be sent to land by an auxiliary ship.

Then the captain asked whether his men might take along their personal belongings.

"We are not pirates," Commander Thierfelder answered. "Let each man get his goods together and bring them to our deck. Every man shall be protected in the possession of his belongings."

The captain communicated this to his officers who in turn passed the word along to the crew.

But Commander Thierfelder had not comprehended the effrontery of these Englishmen. When the transfer of personal belongings began, we found to our surprise that the men claimed almost everything aboard the ship. They wanted to bring off everything movable they could lay hands on. We finally had to set up a court of arbitrament to decide what were lawful belongings and what were not.

The crew of forty-six men thus came aboard the *Kronprinz,* growling and complaining, while we dispatched a part of a division to man the ship.

Our men now began to make interesting discoveries. First, they found hidden in the officers' cabins of the *Potaro* a dozen brand-new revolvers, all loaded with ugly-looking dum-dum bullets. We kept these bullets as evidence and souvenirs.

Second, and most important, charts were discovered which gave the positions of the eighty Allied war vessels at that time searching the seas for us. These charts were exactly what we wanted and were to make our efforts at dodging the enemy much easier.

The splendid Marconi wireless outfit, which the British had not had the wit to destroy when they surrendered, was for the present left on board to be taken down later and installed on our ship.

Orders were now given to the *Potaro* to steam out of sight for the present, so the ship got up eight- to ten-mile speed and was soon over the horizon.

Commander Thierfelder was now on the lookout for big game. He had information which led him to believe large ships not far off. On Wednesday at 8 A. M. we sighted two sailing vessels but let them pass, even changing our course so as not to come too near them. We could not afford to be disturbed by "small fry."

Thursday, the fourteenth of January, the expected prize came. At ten in the morning a three-master had come in sight and the *Kronprinz Wilhelm,* true to her purpose not to be disturbed by small vessels, had altered her course so as to keep out of view. Forty-five minutes later we sighted a large steamer with one smokestack, and, putting on eighteen-mile speed, rapidly neared her. The steamer, a vessel of more than seven thousand five hundred tons, at first looked so much like a war vessel that all hands got ready for battle. On nearer approach, however, we found her to be a freight and passenger liner. As the steamer now refused to stop at our command, we fired a blank shot, whereupon she at once ran up the British flag and came to a halt.

As we came still nearer, our men saw with the naked eye what only a few of us had hitherto noticed with the aid of glasses—that passengers, crew, officers, and even the captain were rushing about in all directions, frantically putting on life-belts and getting together little bundles of belongings.

When later on we asked them why they had done this they gave the usual answer that they had been told that German commerce raiders always sank captured vessels— passengers, crew, and all—without bothering to be humane. We laughed heartily over this, asking who had said it. Oh, they answered, it was a matter of common knowledge. The British papers were full of such atrocities every day. When later we took them on board, men and women looked at us with a kind of demure and mute thankfulness as if we had for some reason accorded their ship a special grace denied to others.

The prize was the *Highland Brae* of London, on her way from England to Buenos Aires, carrying twenty-six steerage and twenty-five cabin passengers in addition to her crew of ninety men. Amongst the passengers were many women and children.

When the *Highland Brae* came to a stop, we sent over a prize crew which ascertained that the cargo of the vessel consisted of two thousand tons of bunker coal, great quantities of gun metal, considerable stores of miscellaneous provisions, and a hodgepodge of general articles of clothing, such as silks, hats, and furs. In addition, she carried about five hundred tons of fresh water, much needed by us. We afterward also found in the cargo thousands of tennis

Three rammings were necessary to sink the WILFRID M.

balls and football pigskins destined for wealthy South Americans.

The *Highland Brae,* built in 1910, was a large ship which stood high out of the water, in every way handsome and seaworthy. Her bridge was equipped with wireless, which the crew had been too frightened to use.

When our prize crew had finished its investigation and returned, the captain of the *Highland Brae* was commanded to steam on ahead of us. Meanwhile, the three-masted sailing vessel, which we had avoided at ten o'clock in the morning, had again come in sight. Thinking us English and being overcome with curiosity, she now bore down upon us, all sails set.

Seeing things thus wilfully come his way, our commander let the schooner draw near. Our prize boat with two officers then put over toward the little craft, refraining, however, from showing our flag. Once aboard the schooner, our officers learned that she wanted to sell us provisions. They inspected her cargo of cod and potatoes, and still not revealing their nationality, were told that the *Wilfrid M.* of Bridgetown (Barbados) was bound for Bahia.

Our officers then revealed their nationality, took captain and crew prisoners of war, and ordered them aboard our vessel. The little crew was dumbfounded but had to obey.

We now came alongside and at once began unloading the schooner. It took only a short time to empty her hull. Then we stood off to ram her and with a slow poke amidships cut her completely in two. A mast, however, still stood upon the stern fragment, so we rammed this half again, destroying it at one blow. The bow half was now floating on its port side, keel above water. This portion we also demolished with a blow. To finish the work we once more ran over the wreckage and then steamed away.

As we were thus giving the little schooner over to destruction, we again noted on board the *Highland Brae* the greatest consternation. All hands had gathered at the rail anxiously watching us. When we began ramming the *Wilfrid M.*, a great wail went up from the women on board the *Highland Brae*. They thought the same fate awaited them. Some we saw hugging their children to them, while others were kneeling on the deck praying. Our commander, being a man of soft heart, brought the *Kronprinz* nearer and had us megaphone over and make signs to the effect that they need have no fear. This somewhat allayed their anxiety, but crew as well as passengers nevertheless watched us warily.

The *Highland Brae* continued steaming along at our side until 5 P. M., when we took her upon our port and gave passengers and crew second-class cabins in our stern. A look of profound relief came over their faces when they saw to what trouble we were going to make them comfortable. Some of the women who had been in hysterics calmed down and thanked us profusely, while others fell to coquetting with our crew.

Our men, who were under orders to treat prisoners of war with utmost civility, now did their duty with the greatest gallantry, the pretty, distressed women and the cute children all getting their share of willing attention. The children were shortly treated to ice cream and cake prepared especially for them under the eye of our chef —an unexpected and welcome treat—and the women were soon presented with needlework made by some of our men. These concrete signs of hospitality changed the suspicious terror of our prisoners to genial confidence. They one and all began to treat the whole affair as a splendid adventure and only hoped they would soon be sent home to correct the false impressions which the outside world cherished against us. Many months later, when we were no longer on the high seas, some of these same passengers wrote letters thanking us for our courtesies to them while on our ship.

Crew and passengers of the *Highland Brae* at last comfortably stowed on our ship, we sent over a division of our crew to man the vessel which at once let go and steamed along at our side. Next day, those of our crew who were still aboard us had to be put through military drill to sober them after their excess of gallantry to the captured women.

We now had on board 219 prisoners of war from the ships *Hemisphere, Wilfrid M., Potaro,* and *Highland Brae.* These people got along very well together, with the exception of those from the *Potaro* who were for the most part clannish and unsociable. The rest had as comfortable accommodations as they could wish and had no complaints

to make. The men from the *Potaro,* however, still had
fault to find. The food was bad, the beds hard, the water
"filthy stale," and the deck space reserved to them for
their airing "nasty." In short, they grumbled about everything we did to make them comfortable.

We were soon to be rid of the complainers. Measures
were being taken to set up additional cabin fixtures aboard
the *Holger* to accommodate the additional prisoners. Then
toward evening of the ninth of January, while this work
was going rapidly on, we left the friendly vessel and the
Highland Brae to their separate tasks and steamed off in
search of the *Potaro,* from which we had not heard since
she left us.

Chapter XVI

LEISURE, A BIRTHDAY, A MILITARY FUNERAL, AND A PARTING

OUR race in the dark in search of the *Potaro* was to prove futile. We steamed steadily onward at a speed of twenty miles, keeping the sharpest lookout. When darkness fell, our watch was doubled. But at one-thirty, finding no trace of the missing vessel, we again turned about and steamed back to the *Holger* and the *Highland Brae,* coming up with them early in the morning.

For the next few days preparations aboard the *Holger* went on rapidly. Meanwhile, we brought the *Highland Brae* on our port and began taking on coal, provisions, and liquors, pumping into our tanks most of the ship's fresh water. As our prize still held a valuable miscellaneous cargo, we had to take especial care lest any of our crew slip over to the vessel's decks during the night and help themselves. A guard was set up along the port promenade deck, and a strict watch was kept for petty thieves. Despite these precautions, we afterward discovered articles on the *Kronprinz* which the men had managed to steal. The crew did not seem to regard this sort of marauding as dishonourable, explaining that the goods would all probably go to the bottom anyway, sooner or later.

By Saturday, the twenty-fourth of January, we had taken from the *Highland Brae* fresh water, wine, beer, seltzer water, champagne, forty boxes of shoes, and great quantities of cloth and articles of clothing. In addition, we had dismantled the ship of all gear and equipment which might be of use to us. To facilitate coaling, we had sent over to the *Highland Brae* our whole third division with all available coaling sacks. We had then let go and steamed away, followed by the *Highland Brae,* whose crew was kept busy filling the sacks and bringing them on deck. Our own crew was set to cleaning and repairing the ship. Among the repairs necessary were some to the boat's deck, where one of our lifeboats had been crushed to splinters by a boom from the *Highland Brae* when the latter vessel plunged against our side in a heavy sea.

While we were thus steaming along at a twelve-mile speed, the sea gradually became rougher, the wind soon rising to such a gale that we could not think of stopping to take on coal. So, to make use of the idle time, Commander Thierfelder had the whole crew of the *Kronprinz* organized into a tailor group. Each man was given his share of blue and gray cloth taken from the *Highland Brae,* and this he cut into the proper shape and then sewed into pantaloons. As I said before, a sailor is usually good at using the needle. Our men made regulation trousers in which they were soon afterward inspected, making a splendid showing. After wearing old clothes so long, the change was indeed refreshing.

The weather at this time became sweltering hot to the discomfort of all on board.

"The bloody sun at noon
Right above the mast did stand
No bigger than the moon."

The men swore about the heat, did away with superfluous clothing, and tried to keep out of the sun, but still the tropical blaze beat fiercely down. On deck in the shade, it is true, a man could still manage to be comparatively comfortable, but below decks, in the engineroom and fireroom, heat was literally infernal.

The *Highland Brae* all this while was following in our wake. Aboard her our men had got the coal into sacks upon deck, ready for transfer as soon as the sea should become calmer. Luckily, the wind settled rapidly, so that by the twenty-ninth weather and sea were once more favourable to coaling.

Early in the morning of that day the *Highland Brae* was brought on our port, and the ready bags and baskets of coal were hoisted from her deck. At nine in the morning, as this work was progressing, the missing *Potaro* put in her appearance on the horizon and was soon again at our side.

Coaling from the *Highland Brae* continued with utmost rapidity, coming to an end next day at 5 P. M. All that then remained to be done was to send the splendid vessel to the bottom.

The sinking of the *Highland Brae* was one of the most interesting as well as spectacular sinkings I witnessed on the whole cruise. At 5 P. M., immediately after the last bag of coal had been hoisted upon our deck, the seacock crew was sent down into the *Highland Brae* to open her cocks. As the *Kronprinz Wilhelm* backed away from the sinking ship, a cable, which was still kept fast to prevent her capsizing before our men could get off, snapped with a noise like the report of a cannon, frightening the women prisoners and making those of our crew off duty in their hammocks start from sleep and rush upon deck. The *Highland Brae* immediately listed to port, sinking rapidly to a certain point, then with increasing slowness. It was not until eight in the evening that her railing was awash.

The night was an ideal one. The full moon sailed high in the heavens, lighting up the sea as though it were day. A hundred yards to port the doomed vessel lay, almost motionless, a continuous grumbling and booming sounding from her hold, where the water was trying to drive out the imprisoned air. At eight-thirty the booming changed to a muffled sighing, sometimes turning to an unearthly whistle.

All hands off duty were on deck to see the end. Suddenly a blast of steam and fire shot up from the prize, followed by the terrific thunder of an explosion, and the ship settled and disappeared under the surface.

Hardly had the *Highland Brae* gone under, however, when she seemed to come up again. Almost immediately a huge hulk appeared on the surface at the spot where the ship had gone down, and after a moment's pause began ploughing rapidly toward us. What to make of this unexpected visitation nobody knew until suddenly the black object sent a thin spout of water high into the air, and our men with a breath of relief cried: "Whale!"

A large whale, unfortunate enough to be under water near the sinking vessel and doubtless stunned by the explosion of the ship's boilers, had come angrily to the surface, where it stayed puffing and blowing a few minutes before submerging itself again.

The *Highland Brae* thus sent to the bottom, the *Kronprinz Wilhelm* steamed off, followed by the *Potaro,* whose turn to go down would come in due course unless the sudden appearance of an enemy warship should disturb Commander Thierfelder's plans. Aboard the *Potaro* our Third Division was occupied as it had been on the *Highland Brae,* filling sacks with coal and bringing them upon deck ready for transfer to the *Kronprinz Wilhelm.*

Meanwhile, the weather had become better. On Sunday, the thirty-first of January, we were steaming in a southwesterly direction at a speed of twelve miles. The day was ideal, a sweet scent in the air, and every outlook splendid. At 4 P. M. the band played on the promenade deck and the men enjoyed the Sunday afternoon with their usual games and naps.

On Tuesday of the following week, as our ship was steaming leisurely along at a twelve-mile speed, we sighted a sailing vessel. Commander Thierfelder, however, did not intend to be interrupted at this time. He knew from wireless warnings that we were in the neighbourhood of enemy warships and did not want to risk being discovered. He accordingly increased the speed of the *Kronprinz* and got out of sight of the schooner. The same thing was done next morning when we sighted a second bark.

While we were thus steaming steadily along, our commander made use of the idle time to parcel out captured shoes, each of our 454 men receiving a new pair. These shoes had been taken as part of the cargo of the *Highland Brae*. The men seemed as proud of them as schoolboys, squeaking valiantly along deck to "break them in." Occasionally we were treated to the spectacle of a "swap" when two men tried to better their "fits" by exchanging shoes. Such exchanges were hailed by onlookers as a good time to stand around and make remarks. One pair of shoes went overboard as a result when a seaman lost his temper at the remarks and flung the pair at the head of the jibers.

On Wednesday, the third of February, our position had become relatively secure and the weather favourable, so we took the prize alongside and began hoisting over the bags of coal. At 5 P. M., while engaged in this work, we again sighted a sail on the horizon, perhaps the same we had seen during the morning, so, having the time, we let go the *Potaro* at five-fifteen and steamed over to investigate the bark.

The ship proved to be a square-rigged sailing ship with

tall masts and large sails—the *Semantha,* of Lyngnor, Norway. The *Semantha* had sailed from Hamburg on January 29, 1914, had departed from Tydestrand, Norway, on the eighteenth of February, had touched at Callao, Chile, on the eighteenth of August, had reached Portland, Oregon, in October, and left there on October fourteenth for Falmouth, England. Her cargo consisted of thirty-six hundred tons of grain.

When our prize crew reported the contraband, the far-travelled ship was declared forfeit, and her crew of twenty-three was ordered aboard us as prisoners of war to be quartered with the rest of our prisoners in the stern, second class.

A little excitement now brightened the early hours of the night. Unlike her predecessors, the brave *Semantha* was given a military funeral. In short, we made a target of her. At nine in the evening, the *Kronprinz Wilhelm* steamed away a distance of six hundred metres and then opened fire with both her guns. It was beautiful to see the shot trail through the night like swift Roman candles and explode on the distant ship. Fifteen rounds were fired—eight shell and seven incendiary. Although the distance was small, darkness made our aim difficult. The boat, however, showed many hits, broke into flames, and burned until the morning, when it sank from sight.

We now steamed back in search of the *Potaro,* which we met next day, and brought the ship alongside at once. Two days of exceptionally rapid and trying work followed.

Coal, provisions, fresh water, cabinet fixtures—everything of value, in short—had to be taken over with utmost celerity, for news had just come by wireless which showed that we were in danger of surprise by hostile warships. Just on the other side of the horizon the *Kronprinz Wilhelm's* enemies lay. If any motive brought them thirty miles nearer, they would sight us.

It cannot be too strongly emphasized how serious an encounter with an enemy warship would have been. For the *Kronprinz Wilhelm,* with her two small guns and her spare supply of ammunition, would be shot down almost without reply as soon as she came within range of a hostile warship. If by chance she should prove fast enough to escape, her position and direction would be wirelessed to all hostile craft, so that sooner or later, once discovered, the armed ring of the enemy must close in.

Commander Thierfelder was therefore so anxious to hasten the work on the *Potaro* that he took personal charge of the operations of coaling and provisioning. The day was sweltering hot, the sea as smooth as a mirror. In the shade the thermometer registered 110 degrees. Our men worked silently in the withering sun, courageously doing their duty, too hot even to grumble, while Commander Thierfelder walked from station to station, speaking to the men, encouraging them to do their best.

Between six and eight that evening, all hands were given a rest, after which the first and third divisions took up the work, while the second and fourth got some sleep.

At nine o'clock, operations were momentarily brought to a halt by an accident to one of our men. A sailor working on the deck of the *Kronprinz* got his foot caught in the tackle of an empty coaling basket. It was night time, and the rattle of chains, the shouts of the men, and the engines made such a deafening roar that the cries and gesticulations of the entangled seaman were not noted. Before anyone knew what was happening, the unfortunate man had been hoisted in mid-air from the basket by his feet and was swung, head dangling downward, from the *Kronprinz Wilhelm's* side and pitched some fifty feet upon the iron deck of the *Potaro*. When we picked him up, his leg and three of his ribs were broken. In fact, it was a wonder that he was not crushed to death. He was immediately carried to the hospital, his injuries were treated, and every care was taken of him thereafter.

Coaling, for the moment interrupted, then went on again as if nothing had happened. At eleven o'clock that hot night, the first and third divisions were in turn relieved by the second and fourth, and by two-thirty o'clock next morning everything was clear and the steamer ready for sinking.

Our seacock squad went down into the vessel, opened the seacocks, and clambered safely upon our decks, whereupon we steamed backward from the sinking ship. The *Potaro* began to go down slowly. It was still above water at four in the morning but a few minutes after six blew up with a tremendous crash and disappeared.

The *Potaro* sent to the bottom, off we steamed to the northeast in search of more prey. Next day, at four-thirty in the afternoon, a sailing ship came over the horizon. We at once steamed over, only to learn that she was an Italian bark, *Rosa M.* of Genoa. The *Rosa M.* had a half-dozen fox terriers aboard which ran along behind the rail in a pack barking furiously at us. This aroused the sympathy of our own dogs, of which there were some fifteen, and all set up a tremendous barking, bellowing, and howling such as the tropical Atlantic had never heard before. The fracas, however, did not last long, for as soon as we were satisfied that the *Rosa M.* was neutral we let her proceed.

A big day for the *Kronprinz* now dawned. Monday, the eighth of February, was Captain Grahn's birthday, and all hands anticipated a holiday filled with sports. So, true to expectations, after the ship had been cleaned, all hands were set free in celebration of the anniversary.

The first event of the afternoon was the raffling off of 454 presents among 454 men, so that each got something. Then followed a moving picture show.

Oh, that show!

It so happened that when the cargo captured from the *Highland Brae* had been examined our men had come upon some motion-picture war films. This discovery brought the demand that the pictures be shown. But, alas! there was no picture machine on board. Not daunted, however, our crew straightway set to work to construct one.

Some of the machinists made a metal box into which

our electricians fitted arc lights. Bicycle sprockets and wheels captured from the *Bellevue* were then put to use, and in short time a motion-picture apparatus was in working condition.

That afternoon of Captain Grahn's birthday all hands who could be packed into the main dining hall were crowded before a canvas screen. When the pictures began to run, all of one accord rose from their seats and shouted the valorous "hurrah!" Verily, for the moment the men thought themselves back in their home cities.

The pictures themselves were not calculated to afford a German crew much delight, but manipulated as they now were they gave the most exquisite pleasure. The scenes, laid in Belgium, ostensibly showed the German armies marching forward, entering villages, plunging swords into women and children, and generally acting the parts of soulless villains. Had these pictures been run as their makers had intended, there would have been a riot.

This is what was done. The pictures, it will be understood, had of course been posed for; even a French audience would have understood that they were not taken from actual action. Now, in the sham work of acting out such scenes, dummy women and children had been substituted for the living actors at the critical moments when bayonets were about to be plunged into them. Later the dummies were replaced by the actors who went through the motions of dying.

As the pictures were now shown, the machine was stopped

whenever a dummy was reached, the straw-stuffed, painted women and children, impaled on the points of swords, being thus left a few moments motionless on the screen. Thus manipulated, the deception was so plain and the incongruity so striking that the pictures became ludicrous, causing continuous merriment. In order that there might be no possibility of mistake, one of the ship's officers stood upon a table to the right of the screen, and, using a cane as a pointer, explained the dummy manipulations in characteristically German scientific fashion.

The dress and actions of the supposed German soldiers also became the butts of the jokes of our critical crew, all of whom knew the real German soldier and his habits too well to be deceived. Half of the supposed German soldiers in this moving picture would have been hooted out of public life for one tenth of the unmilitary bearing which these actors showed.

On the whole the war pictures, which in Allied lands would have made a person's blood boil, gave the German crew of the *Kronprinz* as happy an afternoon as they had had in a long time.

To crown all, the *Kapitän's Geburtstagszeitung*—Captain's Birthday Newspaper—was issued—the third newspaper of the voyage. When the men came out after the moving-picture show, they received their copies and amused themselves over the four-page sheet for the rest of the evening.

Next day, Tuesday, the ninth of February, when the

birthday excitement had again died down and we were steaming toward a point at which we would meet the steamer *Holger,* the commander announced that all men over thirty-nine years of age would be given an opportunity to receive their honourable discharges, go aboard the *Holger,* and so be transported to safety. A great self-questioning at once took place among the older men. Some thought it their duty to stay on the *Kronprinz;* others had dependents at home and thought it best to leave. They talked the matter over with each other, arguing back and forth. Finally, it was apparent that most of them had reached a decision. Those who had decided to stay looked a little prouder and smiled upon everyone; the others went about looking doubtful, not knowing how their act was going to be taken, but nevertheless glad at heart that the long anxiety and nerve strain would soon be at an end.

On Wednesday we slowly proceeded toward the *Holger,* reaching her at 6 P. M. The sea had gradually grown rougher, and the sky was lowering. On Thursday weather and sea were worse, so that it was impossible to take the *Holger* alongside. The steamer, therefore, continued to accompany us at a slow speed.

It was on this day that some boys, our prisoners of war, being told that all prisoners were soon to leave the ship, asked to see our commander. When brought to him, they begged to be allowed to stay aboard our ship after the other prisoners had gone. They wanted to join us and take part in the "fun" of capturing vessels.

When Commander Thierfelder told them it would be treason on their part to fight against their own countries, the scapegraces answered that they merely wanted to see the fun and were willing not to fight if we would only let them stay. The commander good-naturedly laughed but told them to be good boys and go along with the *Holger*. Later on in life, he assured them, they would all grow up to be a credit to their nation, perhaps great naval officers. And to offset their disappointment he imparted as a kind of secret that, as the *Holger* was a German ship, they would stand in hourly danger of being chased and captured. They would most likely see action enough before they got home. With this reassurance the youthful fire-eaters calmed down and returned to their quarters.

On Friday, the sea had become smooth enough to allow the *Holger* to come on our port. The transfer of the prisoners of war—252 in all, collected from the steamers *Hemisphere, Highland Brae,* and *Potaro,* and the sailing vessels *Wilfred M.* and *Semantha*—was now begun.

The departure of these prisoners was somewhat sad. Most of them had made friends with our crew and consequently looked upon their leaving as almost a calamity. For the prisoners had on the whole been a source of comfort.

Especially had this been the case with respect to the captured children. These tots worked themselves into the hearts of our men, many of whom were themselves fathers with children of similar ages at home. The men on their part had done all in their power to be amusing. Some had performed acrobatic feats for them; others had made toys, such as jumping jacks and tops, and showed the children how to play new games. Our ex-comedian Scholke had frequently been permitted to go into the prisoners' quarters to make the children laugh; there he became not only the hero of the little ones, but of the grown-ups as well. His humour was as irresistible to foe as to friend.

The *Kronprinz,* furthermore, officially presented the captured children with ice cream and cake twice a week—on Thursdays and Saturdays. This treat was always awaited with anxiety lest it fail to come and hailed with ecstasy when it arrived. Nothing, in fact, did more to keep the prisoners in good humour than this semiweekly treat to the children.

When, now, the prisoners got together their effects to leave for the *Holger,* the children of one accord set up a chorus of lamentation. They did not want to leave the ship which gave them so much fun and such good treats. Not until they had been assured that they would be given ice cream and cake aboard the *Holger* just as with us were they quieted. Most of them said good-bye with tears in their eyes, and, as on such occasions the softer emotions are contagious, the women used their handkerchiefs freely.

Those of our crew who had decided to leave our vessel were now called on deck. Seventy-three in all—twelve officers, among them our former merchant commander, Captain Grahn, and sixty-one petty officers and men—came forward ready. They had their belongings packed and were nervous to have the parting over. Before they left the ship, however, the commander addressed them, thanking them for their faithful work under his command, reassuring them that they were not unpatriotic in leaving him as his ship was well supplied with men and he wanted to put no unnecessary burden upon those whose age deserved a rest. Thus cheered with handshakes, parting greetings, and requests to be remembered at home if they ever got there, the small contingent went down our ladders.

As the *Holger* put off from our side, a great cheering went up from our prisoners of war who had come to the rail and were waving us farewell. The men waved their hats in the air; the women, their handkerchiefs, which many of them also put to their eyes. They had indeed struck up a friendship with us—these strangers.

The *Holger* steamed somewhat in advance. As we now put on speed and came alongside, our crew gave three cheers for Captain Grahn. Hardly had the roar died down when from the departing *Holger* rose three hearty cheers for Commander Thierfelder. Then came well wishes on the part of the Holger for our continued success until the sounds were lost in the wind as our ship sped past and away. Soon the people at the rail had become so small in the distance that we could not make them out, and in half an hour the *Holger* with her precious wards was over the horizon behind us.

Chapter XVII

THE "GUADELOUPE"—THE GREATEST PRIZE OF THEM ALL

IT WAS the twelfth of February that we parted from the *Holger*. During the next ten days our life was one of continuous drill and routine. We steamed slowly along in a northeasterly direction, painting ship, mending machinery, and caulking leaks, ever mindful of our broken propeller-shaft well.

Our men, in fact, were beginning to show signs of nervous strain. During the last few weeks no war news had reached us, this continuous silence causing noticeable depression among the crew whose whole hearts were with their brothers in the trenches. In the course of the day, I often came upon a group arguing excitedly about the best way to take Paris, or to break the Russian lines and encircle Poland, or some other strategy—denoting the intense interest the men felt in the operations on land. After overhearing some of these discussions, which were often as intense as if the men had been on opposite sides of the war, I could not help thinking of Commander Thierfelder's words in a speech of some weeks before: that, if the men on land were as anxious about the outcome of the war as their comrades were out here on the sea, Germany could hold off her enemies forever.

During the nights of the nineteenth and twentieth we steamed in circles four or five miles in circumference, making about twenty-seven round trips a night. This kept us in the same neighbourhood—an area which Commander Thierfelder rightly thought would afford him a prize—and yet gave us a chance to survey more of the horizon than if we had rested quietly in the same spot.

On Monday, the twenty-second of February, George Washington's Birthday, while we were thus waiting, like Micawber, for something to turn up, our lookout at 2 P. M. sighted the smoke of a steamer on the horizon. "Clear for action!" sounded and we at once steered toward the vessel at a fifteen-mile speed, reaching her at two-thirty.

The steamer, however, refused either to stop or show her flag, so we fired a blank shot with each of our bow guns, whereupon the stranger ran up the British flag and came to a halt. It was the single-funnelled steamer *Chasehill* of London.

The *Chasehill* was a fair-sized vessel, built with a bowsprit like a sailing ship. Upon her black funnel was painted a large white disk, in the field of which lay a conspicuous red cross. Although the *Chasehill* was by no means a hospital ship, or otherwise ship of mercy, she was the only vessel painted with a red cross which we met on the voyage, and, curiously, she proved to be the only captured prize which the *Kronprinz Wilhelm* did not sink. For the *Chase-*

hill was later sent to shore, manned by her own crew, with all our prisoners of war.

Clemency was granted the *Chasehill* not only because of the painted red cross upon her funnel. The vessel, in short, was lucky enough to have accommodations for passengers and was therefore an excellent transport, which fact decided her fate.

Our crew, which had at once rowed over to the prize to get particulars, learned that the *Chasehill* had left London for La Plata with a cargo of three thousand tons of coal, having in addition to this supply fifteen hundred tons still in her bunkers. Her officers and crew of forty-three men were then ordered over to us, and a part of our crew under the command of one of the older officers was sent over to man the vessel. The captured steamer then picked up her speed in our wake.

Things now began to happen rapidly. On Tuesday, the twenty-third of February, which was Commander Thierfelder's thirty-first birthday, all hands expected a holiday given over to sports—excitement. But the wheel of fortune turned other than we expected.

Shortly after dawn of that day, a large steamer with two smokestacks appeared on the northern horizon. It was indeed Commander Thierfelder's lucky day, for this steamer proved the richest prize of the voyage. "Clear for action!" sounded, all hands came to station, and we steamed rapidly down on the enemy.

So large was the distant ship and so bold were her actions

that we began to think we were at last to fight a man-of-war. For a time, the suspense was intense, and everyone made ready for a fight to a finish. As we came nearer, however, the vessel made no preparation for battle which puzzled us until we saw that she was not a war vessel after all. Like her predecessor, she refused either to stop at our signal or to show her flag. We, accordingly, fired a shot across her bows, whereupon the vessel slowed down and ran up the French flag.

It was a large, beautiful freight and passenger vessel, the *Guadeloupe* of Havre. Above her graceful black hull her long white cabin space lay comfortable and roomy. Even her two red smokestacks, banded with black at the tops, had a contented appearance. When the *Kronprinz* had come near enough to ascertain the splendid proportions of the prize, our officers of one accord came up to congratulate Commander Thierfelder. It was indeed the finest birthday present the commander could have wished.

As our prize boat was now rowing over toward the *Guadeloupe,* we noticed a scuffle on the decks of the prize. A number of sailors had run out of one of her cabins carrying three black leathern trunks, weighted with iron, which they now unceremoniously cast into the sea. Two at once went to the bottom; the third, however, remained afloat and was fished up by the two boats which immediately put out from our side for this purpose.

On opening this trunk we found valuable documents and writings addressed to the French Minister of War. In

Commander THIERFELDER *and the* GUADELOUPE, *the richest prize of the cruise. It was taken on the commander's thirty-first birthday.*

addition, there were millions of dollars' worth of checks and drafts payable at Parisian banks, and though this paper was naturally of no use to us our men at least enjoyed the feeling of having captured something valuable.

The prize crew returned with the information that the *Guadeloupe,* which had come from Buenos Aires by way of Montevideo and was bound for Havre via Bordeaux, carried 294 passengers, first, second, and third class. During her flight the *Guadeloupe* had not dared use her wireless, fearing that if we heard her calls for help we might shoot her down bag and baggage.

We were now in a hurry to steam from the spot, so Commander Thierfelder stationed two armed patrols upon the ship and commanded her to follow us. At 4 P. M., we again came up with the *Chasehill,* when we took the *Guadeloupe* on our port and ordered her passengers and crew upon our decks.

This transfer of passengers proved quite a spectacle. As stated, there were 294 persons on the vessel, including many women and a few children. Among the women were some pretty French girls, all about sixteen years old and dressed in the most chic styles. Our crew stared at these goddesses from a respectful distance until the fair ones were corralled out of sight. Then our men made it their business to besiege the prisoners' quarters to get on speaking terms with the girls.

We now began taking over all the baggage of the *Guadeloupe*—a tedious and prolonged process, as the vessel seemed to be stuffed with luggage from stem to stern. At 7 P. M., when the work was finished, we sent thirty of our crew to man the ship and then, letting go, drifted in her neighbourhood all night.

At six o'clock next morning all hands were up and work was begun. Once more we brought the *Guadeloupe* on our port, taking on fresh water, provisions, articles of clothing, tobacco, cigarettes, beer, and meat.

During the morning, as the work was progressing, a sudden swell of the sea brought the starboard deck of the prize against our side with such violence that her whole upper deck was shattered, the noise of the crash and the sudden jolt sending terror to the hearts of our feminine prisoners.

A little later on this day we discovered in the hold of the *Guadeloupe* a large consignment of French colognes. I remember such names as "Ed. Piver," "La Rose France," and "Chevalier d'Orsey." This booty was straightway claimed by our shrewd barber who stocked his room with the bottles and offered them for sale to our crew at an exorbitant price—considering their mode of acquisition. But, before he got far in this profiteering, he noticed his stock unaccountably diminishing. Our men, it developed, were not so easily overreached as he had imagined. Feeling that they had an equal right to the captured cologne, they set themselves to obtain by strategy what had not fallen to them as a free gift of heaven. To be sure, it had never occurred to them to want cologne for their private use until now that the barber had a stock of it, which they did not consider rightly his.

As the crew crowded around the bottles in the barber shop, one man after another slipped a bottle unseen into his blouse; or, boldly asking the price of one, suddenly dashed out of the door saying he would pay some other time when more convenient. Against these tactics the barber dared lodge no complaint, knowing that Commander Thierfelder intended the cologne not for sale but for use in his profession.

Our men used this delicate and precious cologne with the extravagance of barbarians, besprinkling their handkerchiefs, their clothes, their beds and pillows, even their whisk brooms and hair brushes. Someone broke a bottle on the port stairs leading to the bridge, lending that stairway a mellow stench hard to walk through. The whole ship, in fact, was filled with the aroma of a lady's boudoir, some parts being rendered literally uninhabitable. The men did not seem to mind the overdose, stretching themselves and yawning in the stench as if they were in the Garden of Eden.

The unloading of the *Guadeloupe's* cargo proceeded rapidly. At five in the afternoon the ship was empty, whereupon we let go, while our temporary crew made everything ready for the sinking. The seacocks of this ship were enormous—the largest we had opened thus far. At six twenty the work of opening them was finished and the last man over the vessel's sides.

The *Guadeloupe* now surprised us by the rapidity with which she went down. By seven-twenty she was half submerged, when an unusually violent explosion occurred in her hold, the débris flying high into the air. Then the ship, enveloped in dense clouds of steam, settled from sight in a boiling sea. Thus the richest as well as the most beautiful of all the *Kronprinz Wilhelm's* prizes went to the bottom.

Shortly afterward the *Chasehill* steamed away for a rendezvous designated by our commander, and we forged slowly ahead at a ten-mile speed.

As we thus departed from the *Guadeloupe,* we made a closer inventory of her passengers and crew. Among the first-class passengers was the Portuguese nobleman, Count Vasco de Orey, who had just married a cousin of King Manuel of Portugal and was even now on his honeymoon. I introduced myself to the count and countess, asking the former if he would not on his return to land write my mother a few lines concerning my safety. When the count later reached home, he kept his word most chivalrously, writing a long, cheerful letter to my mother, telling of the varied travels of the *Kronprinz,* of her continued success and safety, and of the courtesy with which her officers and crew uniformly treated the passengers of captured vessels.

When this letter reached my family, there was great rejoicing. They had not heard a word from me since I left Hoboken in August, 1914, and did not know whether I was alive or dead. They were of course acquainted with the different announcements in the Allied press of the repeated sinking of our ship but had hoped, nevertheless, that this news was not true. As late as the second of January the London *Daily Mail* had announced that the *Kronprinz* lay stranded on the coast of Argentina, the fate of her officers and crew being unknown. This report, like the various preceding ones, had again put my family into acute suspense. But the letter of Count Vasco de Orey gave them later information, for which they devoutly thanked God, as they wrote me afterward.

I, for my part, felt a burden lifted from my breast when the count told me he would write my people about me. It is uncomfortable to cruise about the ocean, not knowing at what moment an ill fate may make food for sharks of one, without one's even being able to send home a last farewell. Some of us had kept diaries, notes, and descriptions of our happenings, which we wanted to publish. A number of the officers and crew, mindful of stories of shipwreck, put last letters into bottles sealed with paraffin; so that if the vessel should be sunk these might float to some favourable shore and reach the world. Of all these expedients, however, the kind memory and good will of Count Vasco de Orey relieved me.

I did all I could to make the count and countess feel at home on our ship. As already noted, all prisoners on the *Kronprinz* had been confined to the prisoners' quarters. At my suggestion, however, Commander Thierfelder made an exception of the count and his bride. The couple was given a first-class stateroom opening on the starboard promenade deck, and they remained the guests of the officers for the rest of their stay on board.

The count was an agreeable companion, particularly obliging in telling reminiscences. One story drew on another; and in the interest of the talk we forgot the sea, forgot the war, and momentarily felt ourselves back again in the free and peaceful days before July, 1914.

The count was especially devoted to his beautiful young wife, always becoming restless when separated from her. We, accordingly, arranged to have the bride at our Wiener Kaffee, where we held our chats; would even, and indeed gladly, have gone so far as to invite other feminine prisoners to keep her company had not Commander Thierfelder prohibited it. The rules of war admitted of one exception —that one being a royal one—but were not elastic enough for two.

I played many a knotty game of chess with the count. The countess preferred the milder excitement of checkers, and, curiously enough, she beat me at almost every game, ever remonstrating that I was not playing in earnest. Be this as it may, it was great fun to watch the countess win.

It must not be inferred from these pleasurable hours we officers had in the company of the titled bridal pair that our days were all holidays. On the contrary, our duties were performed as usual, only the hours off duty being used for hospitalities. As one third of the officers were always off duty, however, the count and countess had continual company.

It was on holidays that the royal pair received most attention. A few such fell during their stay with us, perhaps the most pleasant being the twenty-third of February, when Commander Thierfelder declared a holiday to take the place of the one we had been forced to forego on his birthday.

After a swift cleaning of the ship in the morning all hands were set free and the day and evening given over to diversified celebration. The band played on the promenade deck; the men engaged in sports, games, and reading, while our prisoners of war were regaled with a minstrel show followed by cakes and cream.

To make us feel still more at ease, at 2:30 P. M. the steamer *Chasehill* again came back to us and lay by.

The week that followed was a busy one, coaling from the *Chasehill* taking place daily, except for short periods when the weather was too rough. While coaling, we often rubbed our prize severely. In fact, we had been on the high-sea hunt so long that we were getting a little careless in our management of the prizes. On Wednesday, as the *Chasehill* was steaming up to come alongside, her steering gear got out of order and her rudder refused to obey the helm. The instant Commander Thierfelder noticed this he gave "Full steam astern!" but it was too late to avoid a collision. The jolt of our ships was severe, but luckily no great damage was done, save to the nerves of our prisoners. Repairs on the ship were at once begun and coaling went on as usual.

Commander Thierfelder had now fully made up his mind to use the *Chasehill* for transferring the prisoners back to land. On Saturday, the sixth of March, our second division was sent aboard the vessel to clean her for the accommodation of so many people. These men stayed on the *Chasehill* until Monday, when they were again transferred to the *Kronprinz*. Our ships now separated for the night, the *Chasehill* proceeding over the horizon to the east, while we steamed leisurely to the north. Commander Thierfelder, it developed, expected a prize and wanted the *Chasehill* to act as a scout. The time, however, passed without event, and on Tuesday at 3 P. M. the *Chasehill* steamed back again to our port side.

This was to be our last day together. The baggage of all our prisoners was now transferred to the prize, together with sufficient mattresses, blankets, dishes, etc., and provisions for three days. By seven-thirty the work was finished and the vessel ready to depart.

When the time now came to send over the prisoners of war, the same scene took place which had occurred at the departure of the *Holger,* the children crying because they did not want to leave our ship. They liked our pleasant men, our entertainments, and above all the ice cream which had been given to them as regularly as to their predecessors. At last, however, we persuaded them that in three short days they would be on land again, when they would have everything they wanted.

That evening while the transfer was going on, a discussion took place as to who should command the *Chasehill* on her trip to freedom. The vessel, of course, was to sail under her own crew. Among the prisoners of war, however, were two captains, those of the *Chasehill* and the *Guadeloupe*. The former, an Englishman, thought the command of the ship should be given to him as a matter of right. The captain of the *Guadeloupe,* however, an older man, a Frenchman, had by his continued courtesy made a good impression upon us, so that Commander Thierfelder thought him fitter for the post, and despite the energetic protests of his rival designated him not only commander of the *Chasehill* but her owner.

Count Vasco de Orey and his bride were the last prisoners to leave the *Kronprinz.* When the time came to depart, the count shook us all cordially by the hand and thanked us for our hospitality. I walked with the couple to the gangplank where the count embraced me and took a second leave. Then with a pleasant wave of his hand and a ringing "Good luck!!" he turned away to help his beautiful companion down our gangplank.

Shortly afterward, without a sound of farewell, the *Chasehill* departed. The night was dark and I could not see any soul on her decks distinctly. As I peered from the port rail of our bridge, I imagined I could see two figures, which I thought to be those of the count and countess, standing at the *Chasehill's* rail watching us. Soon, they became indistinct, and I was left to wonder whether I should ever see my pleasant friends again.

The *Chasehill* had an interesting after career. Three days after she left us, she put safely into Pernambuco. There she lay a few months undergoing repairs, while a legal battle took place over her ownership. The French captain of the *Guadeloupe* claimed the vessel as having been given him by the commander of the *Kronprinz Wilhelm,* maintaining that the ship was at the time the rightful property of the *Kronprinz,* taken under the rules of war. The British captain, however, won the case, whereupon the vessel was restored to its former owners.

After this decision of the courts the *Chasehill* took a miscellaneous cargo to New York, where she was loaded to the limit with munitions of war and cleared for England. On the way across she was lost in mid-ocean without trace, most likely broken to pieces in a gale which at that time swept the Atlantic.

The *Chasehill,* as mentioned, was, with the exception of the little Russian schooner, the only captured prize which the *Kronprinz* did not sink. Our crew had wondered not a little that she was spared, thinking it unnecessary to return so large a ship to the Allies. But when the men later learned the vessel's fate, they were glad the commander had let her go, rejoicing that the munitions had gone to the bottom.

On the day after the departure of the *Chasehill,* at 5 P. M., as we were steaming along at a ten-mile speed, we sighted a good-sized steamer, so we increased our speed to fifteen miles and reached the vessel by six o'clock. But as the steamer in customary fashion failed either to stop or show her flag, we fired a shot across her bows, whereupon the Belgian flag was run up and the vessel came to a halt.

Our prize crew at once rowed over, ascertaining the vessel to be the *Anvers* of Antwerp, carrying a cargo of flour, corn, and loam for the Netherlands Trust Company in Rotterdam. These articles were not contraband of war and were destined for a neutral country with the probability of finally reaching Germany. We, accordingly, caused the captain of the vessel to sign papers presented to him, whereupon at eight o'clock that evening we let the vessel go her way.

The *Anvers* steamed off fully lighted, visible for miles in the dark. As she steamed on, thus boldly showing herself, I could not help repeating the thought, though not the words, of Holy Scripture to the effect that the innocent may go unafraid, for they are in the care of heaven.

The *Anvers,* however, was not so lucky as I imagined. A week later, while nearing Europe, she was stopped by a U-boat whose commander, after looking over the *Anvers's* papers, pronounced them unsatisfactory. The captain of the *Anvers* protested that his cargo was actually destined for Germany by way of neutrals, but the U-boat commander shook his head. Then the captain reported his meeting with us, saying that Commander Thierfelder had seen his papers and been convinced that his cargo was destined for neutral consumption. At this the U-boat commander merely smiled and answered that he could not be bound by the decision of other German officers.

The *Anvers* was straightway sent to the bottom and her crew in small boats towed to the vicinity of land. All reached shore safely, where, in their general maledictions upon the U-boat commander, they mingled words of praise for the commander of the *Kronprinz Wilhelm* who had been so polite to them.

It was only a short time after this meeting with the *Anvers,* as we cruised leisurely northward, that Commander Thierfelder ordered all available men to begin painting the outside walls of our ships. Considering the latitude we were in, our direction, and some circumstances which I shall soon mention, I held this to be an important sign.

"Heinz," I said to Hoffmann that evening in my room, "I think our cruise will soon be over. Thierfelder's going to run into a North American port."

"Has he said anything to you about it?" Hoffmann asked quickly.

"Not a word, but everything points that way."

"That's what I've been thinking ever since he sent back the *Chasehill* with the prisoners," my friend agreed. "Then there are the sick men——"

"Six more to-day," I added. "I've just met Fix and he says three beriberis reported at noon inspection."

Hoffmann shook his head.

"It can't last long," was his verdict.

Chapter XVIII

THE FLIGHT NORTH

THE *Kronprinz Wilhelm* had fallen upon ill days. On Commander Thierfelder's birthday, the very day on which the splendid prize, *Guadeloupe,* was taken, two seamen reported sick. Their feet were swollen and the men were too weak to stand. After a brief examination our doctors pronounced the symptoms those of beriberi.

To any who have not seen a patient suffering with beriberi I would state that the disease, which had its origin in a diet poor in fresh vegetable matter, causes a swelling, first of the feet and then gradually of the legs. At the same time the stricken person becomes weak and listless. There *is* only one remedy for the disease—a diet containing mainly vegetable ingredients. Unfortunately, we had no fresh vegetables left on board.

The discovery of this sickness came as a surprise to the crew but not to the officers. For months the men had been living on canned and salt meats, so that the commander was expecting an outbreak of beriberi any day. The day after the first cases were reported a third man was stricken, and next day three more.

To lighten the discomfort of the patients, the men were

confined to their bunks, their swollen legs being bandaged with woollen cloths. When a sick man was seated in a chair, his legs were always propped up so as to be horizontal, since in this position he felt no pain. Complete rest was prescribed for all patients.

At first the sick men lay in their bunks, quite disconsolate. As the number of cases increased, a first-class cabin opening to the starboard promenade deck was converted into a hospital and the men bunked there together. As the number of patients continued to grow a second cabin adjoining the first was added, thus enabling the men to be sociable in their common affliction.

There is nothing, however, which an active man hates more than to be bedridden. Our sick were a sorry spectacle. Not one of them was actually in pain, yet all felt miserably useless.

We consequently did all we could to entertain them. Graphophones were taken from the officers' quarters and placed one in each ward. Then all books and magazines, of which the *Kronprinz* had quite a store, were put at the sick men's disposal, and these went the rounds of the cots. A seaman was detailed to each sickroom to attend to the graphophones, to give the men books, and to read aloud; and members of the crew were encouraged to spend as much of their leisure time as possible with the sick men to keep them in good humour. I had to admire the tact and good sense which Commander Thierfelder showed in this time of trial, and the splendid spirit which the crew displayed toward their helpless brothers.

The knowledge that so many cases of beriberi were occurring naturally had a depressing effect upon the remainder of the crew, each man wondering whether he might not be the next to be stricken, as all were eating the same food.

On March twelfth, just at an opportune time to relieve this depression of spirits, important news arrived by wireless. That afternoon, when all hands had assembled aft, Commander Thierfelder announced that the German Admiralty had bestowed upon him the Iron Cross first class and upon one hundred officers and men the Iron Cross second class. My own name was read with the others as having received the Iron Cross second class.

As was to be expected, this news brought good cheer and renewed determination to officers as well as crew. Their labours in the service of the Fatherland had won official recognition, and they felt that they would deserve still better of their country. The coming of the awards at just this time only clinched my opinion that the end of the voyage was approaching. The award of the medals was merely the official stamp which certified that the *Kronprinz Wilhelm* had done her work and that her cruise was near its end.

But if this was really the case no one would have surmised it from Commander Thierfelder's words or actions. In all matters of importance he continued to preserve a Sphinx-like silence, not a soul aboard ship being his confidant. Far from sharing his plans with us, he kept us guessing as to his intentions until the very day before the end.

If, furthermore, the end of the cruise was approaching, there was not a sign of end of work or of excitement. On Saturday, the thirteenth of March, at twelve o'clock, as the crew was finishing cleaning ship, an S O S came from a Spanish passenger vessel which was on fire. Changing our course we at once steamed full speed in the given direction, warily keeping a lookout, however, lest we be led into a snare. Half an hour later the wireless changed its note, reporting that help was no longer needed, as the fire was under control. We, accordingly, turned about to our former course, relieved to learn that the first message had been sent in good faith.

On that same day we again passed the equator, this for the sixth time, and bore to the north.

"It's the last time we cross the line on this voyage," I remarked to Hoffmann.

He shrugged his shoulders.

"I think we're going to make a port in the United States," he answered.

The third issue of our ocean newspaper appeared that day—this time entitled the *Æquator Zeitung*—Equator News—filled as before with jokes, silly advertisements, and impossible "news." The sheet was particularly welcomed in the hospital room, for the sick men were already bored with our library books and graphophone records.

Coalers—eminently important functionaries on the raider's cruise.

The TAMAR, *captured and sunk in the later days of the cruise.*

The heat at this time was oppressive beyond endurance, for we were in the very heart of the tropics. Our supply of fresh water, furthermore, was beginning to run low, so that Commander Thierfelder altered our course to the west, where we cruised about in the tropical rain districts, catching rain water in sheets of canvas spread out on deck.

As a matter of fact, things were not going well aboard our ship. To sum up the situation, our supply of fresh water was critically low, our bunkers almost empty, our propeller-shaft well was leaking worse than before, and thirty of our men were helpless with the beriberi. To enkindle the flagging spirits of the men, Commander Thierfelder had recourse to *Allemansmanöver*, but even this seemed somewhat lacking in verve.

On Monday, the twenty-second, we were in the singular position of steaming momentarily in a neutral district, so that we could not attack any ships. At 12:30 A. M. we sighted a large steamer but refrained from attacking lest we break the laws of neutrality. At 5:30 P. M., when we were again out of neutral waters, a second steamer appeared, but as it was almost dark and we could not recognize the vessel we did not give chase. Again at ten o'clock that night a third steamer came in view. This vessel was completely illuminated, the inference being that she was neutral, so we let her go her way.

Next morning began propitiously enough. At five-thirty we sighted a small steamer and at once gave chase. But when an hour later we reached the prize, we found her to be the little neutral Italian ship *Italia* of Spezia, voyaging from Palermo to Buenos Aires.

On the following day, Commander Thierfelder was in better luck. At one-fifteen in the afternoon a vessel appeared on the horizon, three points to starboard. Instantly "Clear for action!" sounded and we steamed with a sixteen-mile speed upon the ship. At three o'clock we came within range, when a splendid vessel revealed herself to us.

The ship we were nearing was the *Tamar* of the Royal Mail Steam Packet Company, so famed for its splendidly built and conditioned ships, one of which, the *Potaro,* we had already sent to the bottom. Bridges and cabins of the *Tamar* looked trim and clean, while her yellow funnel, cocked back at a good-natured angle, gave a most hospitable impression. When I got a near view of the *Tamar,* I could not help feeling a pang of remorse that so neat a craft must be sunk.

As we were thus slowly approaching the steamer, suddenly we saw some of her crew tearing up papers and throwing them overboard, so we sent out some boats to fish up the torn fragments. Nothing of importance, however, came to light.

Our prize crew now boarded the *Tamar,* learning that she was of Middlesborough, England, on her way from Santos to Havre with a cargo of sixty-eight thousand sacks of coffee. Among her crew of thirty-three men were seven Malays.

The crew of the *Tamar* admitted that they had not

recognized the *Kronprinz* until the very last moment. Until we had come almost within hail, they had believed us British and had wondered why we did not show our flag. The *Kronprinz,* they said, was the last ship they could possibly have expected to meet, as they had been assured before leaving Santos that the commerce raider had been sunk. They thought it a good joke to be captured by the very vessel they believed to be at the bottom of the ocean.

The crew of the *Tamar* was ordered aboard us, after which we quickly took on fifty sacks of coffee—about all we could expect to use—some provisions, and two living pigs. The seacock crew then opened the ship's cocks.

When the men were safe aboard our vessel, Commander Thierfelder took the *Kronprinz* a short distance away and let the gun crews open fire upon the sinking prize. Six shots in all were sent into the vessel's hull, not one going wild.

The sinking of the *Tamar* was slow; at first it looked as though it were going to take until midnight. At ten in the evening, the ship's boilers blew up with a tremendous explosion—smoke, steam and débris flying high into the air with a shower of sparks which scintillated in the night like a display of fireworks. When the air cleared again, the vessel had disappeared.

The *Tamar* sunk, the *Kronprinz* lost no time in leaving the spot. We were in a sea lane leading to the United States, so that at any moment our presence might be detected. Indeed, our course, though evidently near its end, was soon to be so eventful that some on board for a time wished we had never put to sea.

On Friday, the twenty-sixth of March, at six in the morning we sighted a sailing vessel, reaching her at eight o'clock, only to learn that she was the neutral Norwegian three-masted bark *Gracia* from Christiania.

That afternoon for the sake of variety our ship's guard was given practice in sharpshooting. The men at the large guns had been accustomed to practise without using ammunition. Empty cartridges were used, and when the piece had been pointed only a small rifle attached to it was fired to record the hit.

Our sharpshooters, on the other hand, used regulation ammunition, firing at a target towed from our stern. We officers practised with our peculiar weapon—the revolver. To make the shooting safe, a small target of wood faced with paper, upon which were painted concentric black and white rings, was fastened to a back spear, hinged to the stern bridge. This spear was then swung out over the ship's side, all shots aimed from the bridge at the target thus going away from the ship. When a man had finished his allotted rounds, the back spear was again swung back to the bridge and the hits counted.

But we also shot at bottle targets, throwing the bottles into the air and shooting at them with birdshot before they struck the water, continuing firing at them after they reached the water until they were out of range.

Birds also often became targets. The flying albatross, as

already mentioned, was frequently brought down on the wing, though I personally did not like to see the stupid but good-natured bird shot for sport.

When porpoises or flying Dutchmen or flocks of flying fish were in evidence, we always watched our chance and cracked away at them. Many a red streak tinged the green surface of ocean during our porpoise-shooting, and many a shark made a meal of our victims. The flying fish were naturally hard to hit because of their speedy flight, nor was it possible to tell when a hit had been made, since the fish under ordinary circumstances plunge suddenly into the water.

The shooting that Friday was satisfactory for many reasons. Hoffmann hit the paper bull's-eye three times in succession, and I shot the neck off a bottle in mid-air—a feat which with a single exception was unanimously called an accident. The exception was myself.

Next day, early in the morning, we sighted the Italian steamer *Fede* of Savona, on her way from that city to Montevideo. We exchanged signals with the *Fede* and passed by.

Just a little before eight that evening, the *Kronprinz Wilhelm* had better luck. On the horizon glimmered a light which we took for a neutral ship fearless of revealing her identity. But Commander Thierfelder, taking no chances, ordered "Clear for action!" and steamed over toward the vessel. It was well he did so, for the ship proved to be the British steamer *Coleby* of Stockton, whose cargo of wheat was being carried from Rosaria to St. Vincent. The *Coleby,* a whaleback type steamer of almost four thousand gross tons burden, was not at all a bad prize.

As mentioned, we should never have seen this ship had she not been fully lighted. When asked why their ship did not run in darkness, the crew replied that they apprehended no danger. The *Prinz Eitel Friedrich*—our rival German raider of the Atlantic—had recently put into Newport News, and as for the *Kronprinz Wilhelm,* they had been instructed that she was at the bottom of the ocean, sunk by a British man-of-war. When we later examined the log of the *Coleby,* we found this to be true. The book contained a statement that definite word of our sinking had been received. We now ordered the ship's crew over to us and took on a small supply of provisions by means of boats.

It was interesting to me to see how quickly and without waste of effort the men of the *Kronprinz* now went about the task of preparing the *Coleby* for sinking. Indeed, so accustomed was the crew to its various duties that the work went on like clockwork. In fact, the *Coleby* was the four-teenth ship to be sunk by the *Kronprinz.* A "sinking psychology" had been developed in both officers and men. No longer were there the hesitancy and lack of certainty; no longer the pangs of remorse that had characterized the first sinkings. Each man knew his duty—was used to the steps of destruction. The work progressed like a drill.

The *Coleby* had been halted at 8 P. M., at ten-fifty-five all was ready for her destruction. The *Kronprinz* steamed away a short distance, whereupon her two forward guns were pointed and six shots fired into the water line of the doomed ship. We then waited in the neighbourhood until five-fifteen in the morning, when, after the usual explosion, the vessel went to the bottom.

It was well for us that the *Coleby* went down so soon. Our wireless was at that time in a fever of receiving. Each of our instruments was taking in messages which showed the neighbourhood to be thick with enemy warships, some not forty miles away. Luckily, the night was dark and the *Kronprinz* had the protection and guidance of her "wireless eyes."

When morning dawned, all hands were up, on the lookout for enemy ships, but the horizon was clear. That day, March twenty-eighth, was Palm Sunday—a holiday for all men. The ship proceeded in its northerly course, bent, as I now learned, on meeting the German steamer *Macedonia,* which had left Las Palmas with a cargo of coal and provisions, and which we had been directed by wireless to expect a little north of the equator. Our orders, as now revealed to us, were to coal from the *Macedonia* and then proceed by way of Norway to some German port.

When this news was delivered to the officers, Hoffmann was overjoyed. He could not bear to think of coming into a neutral port to be interned for the rest of the war. Of all patriotic Germans I ever met, Hoffmann was positively the most zealous.

"Now, Niezy," he exclaimed that morning at breakfast, "when we reach Germany we'll be given a chance to enter the submarine service. Think of it, Niezy! To get a chance to blow the 'Mistress of the Sea' off her element."

He had his plans all laid. He would go in training and become commander of a U-boat. This was his one ambition, he said, now that Britain "was trying to conquer Germany by starving her women and children."

At 4 P. M. Hoffmann and I went on watch on the bridge. It was a beautiful afternoon, hot but calm, a clear sky above, with a fiery red sun gradually declining toward the horizon. All on board had enjoyed an exceptionally pleasurable Palm Sunday holiday, while Hoffmann and I, having had a good meal together, were in a truly comfortable mood. Nevertheless, I could see that my friend was a little anxious, for at any moment of our watch we might expect to sight the *Macedonia*—my friend's one hope of getting back to his Fatherland.

I shall never forget that watch. At six o'clock the *Kronprinz* was leisurely steaming westward on the great circle appointed for the rendezvous. The immense red ball of the sun stood blinding us with molten brightness just at the edge of the horizon. So sharp were its rays that it was impossible to look directly that way.

At 6:30 P. M. the lookout suddenly cried: "Smoke on the bow!"

Hoffmann and I, straining our eyes toward the horizon,

The COLEBY, *the* KRONPRINZ'S *fourteenth captive.*

beheld a faint haze. Then all at once my friend seized my arm.

"Niezy," he cried, "look there—there at the sun!"

Shading my eyes with my hand, I strained them toward the horizon. The great molten face of the sun had sunk one half below the sea so that its massive upper arch of gold covered a great stretch of horizon. With a flash the truth came over me. There, outlined against the golden surface of the sun, stood many masts and funnels like thin black prison bars jutting up from the horizon. The unlooked for happened. Some British cruisers had captured the *Macedonia* and all were now lying there in the west against the face of the sun.

In a twinkling Hoffmann sounded the gong; "Clear for action!" rang out, and the ship from a peaceful Palm Sabbath slumber woke to the heat and fever of desperate life.

In a few moments Commander Thierfelder was on the bridge. Taking in the situation at a glance, he commanded "Full speed astern!" and our vessel slowed down, stopped, and began to back to the east, keeping her prow pointed directly toward the sun.

The command given and executed, Commander Thierfelder, his features pale but firm, leaped down the steps of the bridge, crossed the gangway to the forward mast, entered and climbed up to the lookout, from which he did not budge for the next half hour. He sang his commands down to us from the mast top.

The *Kronprinz Wilhelm* continued to travel backward at top speed, making at least twenty miles astern, her firemen working like devils. The one question in our minds was whether we were being seen by the enemy. Evidently, as the sun was in the west and sinking, we made a target of clear observation for the British warships to our west. In truth, I wondered how they could possibly help not seeing us.

But whether they could recognize us or not was another question. It was precisely in order to prevent our being recognized that Commander Thierfelder kept the nose of his ship pointed toward the enemy, backing away with loss of speed instead of turning about and going into full flight at twenty-five miles. So long as we remained bow-on to the enemy the number of our funnels and masts could not be counted. Had he turned about, the British would easily have recognized us while we were broadside to them.

Darkness now came on to our saving. No sooner had the sun sunk and night fallen, which happens almost at the same moment in these latitudes, than Commander Thierfelder came down from the mast top, put the helm about, pointed his ship directly to the east, and steamed at full speed. He kept up this flight to the east for two hours, when he turned to the north and sped on in a zigzag course in this direction for the rest of the night.

During the first hours of this chase the greatest excitement reigned. The Allied warships had been so near that the crew thought their last hour had come. All stood **to** their posts until late in the night, when the command to cease watch was given and all except the regular watch turned in for the night. The prisoners of war were likewise under great excitement. Being seamen, they could tell from the actions of our ship and crew what was happening. Some hoped for our capture, while others as earnestly prayed for our escape, lest an encounter result in the sinking of our ship while they were on board.

When the crew was finally relieved from duty that night, some of the men packed their most precious belongings into bundles; these they secretly stowed into the lifeboats, so that if next day they should be forced to abandon the ship their effects would be saved. We officers, however, were on the lookout for this action. Next morning the lifeboats were searched and the names of the guilty men published. Only a mild reprimand came from the lips of the commander who told the culprits that they should have more confidence in him and a greater sense of justice toward their fellow men of the ship than to make selfish preparations for flight. The revelation of the names afforded matter for many jokes at the expense of the timorous seamen.

When Hoffmann and I came off the watch that night, we went to his room. My friend was a disappointed man.

"No Germany for us," he growled. "We haven't coal enough even to get to the United States."

"Yes," I answered, "we have coal enough for that. I figured out last week that we can make Cape Henry and have about four hundred tons to spare. This extra trip we're taking to-night cuts us down about three hundred tons, so we can still make the capes with a little to spare. Besides, we can make a more southerly port, if necessary."

"Well, I know what I'll do, then," Hoffmann answered.

For should we reach the United States and be interned, my friend was resolved to try at any cost to get back to Germany even if he had to buy a yacht to do so. This, in fact, was ultimately what he did do, and in doing so he lost his life.

The night of northerly flight at last wore away. At dawn all of the crew off duty were on deck to a man, everyone anxious to learn whether the British warships were in chase. Not a trace of the enemy was visible. The men breathed freely again, and Commander Thierfelder once more turned the *Kronprinz* toward the northwest to make for the United States.

From Monday, the twenty-ninth of March, to Sunday, the fourth of April, we steamed along without sighting a single vessel. Then early Sunday morning we came across an American whaler under heavy sail. We only exchanged signals, however, and steamed on. This was the last vessel we saw by day on our cruise on the high seas.

Commander Thierfelder still kept the nose of the *Kronprinz* to the northwest, so that I could tell with certainty that he was heading for the Virginia Capes.

When I was sure this was his intention, I knew there was excitement ahead. Each port of the United States deep enough to permit of our entering, especially the entrance of these Capes, was guarded by a watchful cordon of Allied battleships. Outside this stockade would be a plentiful number of outposts in wireless touch with the blockading squadron. To run the gauntlet of this swarm of enemies seemed an impossibility. But in the eyes of these German seamen nothing was impossible until it had been tried. And now the trial was to be made.

Chapter XIX

THE FINAL DASH—AND SAFETY

ON SATURDAY evening, the tenth of April, the *Kronprinz Wilhelm* had approached to within sixty miles of the Virginia Capes. The night was fairly dark, propitious to our slipping in. Before sundown Commander Thierfelder had called a council of the officers and announced that during the early hours of the night he would make the attempt to dash in.

"There are six cruisers outside the Capes," he said, "but with the help of God we will get through."

He asked us to caution our men, this night of all nights, not to show a light or make an unnecessary noise, and as soon as darkness fell the ship was inspected from stem to stern to locate any chance crevice through which a light might be seen.

While these measures were being taken, the men in the fire and engine rooms were busy trimming, oiling, wiping, and inspecting, taking every precaution against accident in the critical hour.

At last, everything in readiness, "Clear for action!" sounded and all hands went to their posts, from which they were ordered not to stir until we should be safe within the Capes.

The dash thus begun continued at utmost speed, so that we were rushing toward the three-mile limit with every ounce of steam on, ploughing through the Atlantic like a ship before a storm. In the wireless room Lieutenant Brinkmann and his assistants were at their instruments, keeping their ears pricked for any message which might affect our course, while on the bridge and at the mast top the lookouts were straining their eyes for signs of the enemy. On deck all was silence, the men even going to the ridiculous extreme of walking softly, while at the guns the cannoneers stood silent, ready for command.

When the lights of the Capes first appeared a thrill went through me. These lights, the first signs of shore I had seen in many a day, were so welcome they seemed like home. Behind those lights was a haven of safety, a great nation, friendly to both sides in the war, and now our sole hope of protection. Only a short stretch of water lay between us and that land, and we must cross that stretch unseen. For we knew that this space was guarded by enemy guns.

Our ship shot along at a rate that made her tremble like a locomotive. In the fireroom the stokers were working like slaves, the emergency acting as a goad whipping them to action, while we on the bridge were in a cold sweat of suspense watching for enemy lights. As yet we had seen no hostile ships.

Suddenly, while we were still some three miles from the neutral zone, the starboard lights of a cruiser twinkled directly ahead. Commander Thierfelder at once swung the helm around, changing our course slightly to port. Hardly had he done so, however, when a second light, the red port lights of another cruiser, became visible only a mile to the south of the first. Commander Thierfelder readjusted the helm, this time to starboard, then passed the word along to stand at the guns.

Two enemy warships were thus ahead of us, one to the starboard, the other to port, only a mile apart, and between these two ships the *Kronprinz Wilhelm* must make her dash. As mentioned, every ounce of steam was already on. The commander nevertheless called down to the engine room:

"Lay on, men! Now we're going through."

As I stood there in the dark watching the enemy, a thousand possibilities of catastrophe went through my mind. I pictured what would happen if a boiler should burst, a propeller break, the rudder smash, or any of a hundred possible accidents occur. At the same time I was straining my eyes toward the ship to port, while Fix at my side was watching the one to starboard. For a moment I thought I saw a slight change in the cruiser's course, as if it had sighted us and were turning about. But I was mistaken. The cruiser kept on in its slow course toward the north.

Meanwhile, Commander Thierfelder had his ear to the telephone listening to Lieutenant Brinkmann who reported that the British were talking with each other but had not yet sighted us.

The minutes sped. Already we were between the hostile cruisers and dashing down upon the neutral line. A few moments more and, whistling through the night, we shot past the neutral limit into the safe waters of the United States.

Nobody cheered. All was silence. But as the ship coursed along, still at top speed, every man pressed his neighbours' hand. A dangerous period had passed. The *Kronprinz Wilhelm* was safely returned from the sea.

What was the astonishment in Chesapeake Bay when our great hulk was seen steaming in! We ran up our blue lights, sounded our deep-toned whistle, and woke the pilot. He came aboard in amazement. He could hardly believe his eyes. Was it possible that a German ship of our size had run the gauntlet of the enemy battleships posted outside the Capes for no other purpose than to prevent just such craft as ours from getting in?

In truth, we had had a narrow escape. Had the British cruisers been a little more watchful, had they made proper use of their searchlights, had Commander Thierfelder been less adroit or less fearless, surely we should never have gotten into the bay. As it was, we got in just in the nick of time. For when we cast anchor in the bay that night we had only twenty-five tons of coal in our bunkers—an hour's running supply.

The crew, released from command, now fell into ecstasies; some danced, some turned somersaults, and all acted as if possessed. That they would be interned was a foregone conclusion. But it sufficed that the ship was safe, had not been captured, had not been beaten on the sea.

The *Kronprinz Wilhelm* had been a legitimate terror to her enemies and a source of military benefit to her nation. For 251 days she had cruised about, exposed to every inclemency of weather and war, without putting into any harbour. In that time she had stopped twenty-six vessels, fourteen of which, aggregating 58,201 tons, had been sunk. She had covered a distance of more than 37,000 miles— more than one and one half times the circumference of the globe. Such a terror to commerce had she become that every conceivable story was afloat concerning her. Some had seen her in the Indian Ocean as well as in the Pacific, while the Allied press had at five different times pronounced her sunk in as many portions of the globe, the last time in March, 1915, when an English auxiliary cruiser assured the *Tamar* that the *Kronprinz Wilhelm* had long ago been sent to the bottom. Our ship had thus been for 251 days a kind of mystery ship—a world known to ourselves and to ourselves alone. Now once more all hands on board would be merged with the great world outside.

Next day, Sunday, the eleventh of April, was a memorable one. A slight fog lifted early and morning broke in purple and gold. Looking up, we beheld the squadron of the American fleet drawn up in line in the bay, while a glance to the ocean showed us the gray forms of the disappointed Allied warships past which we had run in the night.

At seven in the morning a United States launch put out to our side, sending aboard two compliment officers to make arrangements for paying the official respects of the United States government upon our arrival. Then at eight, we weighed anchor and steamed up the bay. As we came abreast the United States' ships, our crew lined the decks, standing at salute.

Now the first guns of the American vessels boomed out in salute, one by one until each ship had fired. Then the bands of the battleships began playing "Heil dir im Sieger-kranz," one picking up the tune as the last finished it. "The Star Spangled Banner" followed, pulsating across the bay until we had passed the whole review, when our men dropped their salute and lined the rail, waving and cheer-ing in return to the American sailors. For by agreement our guns had not answered the American salute, as we were without ammunition. Shortly afterward we cast anchor to await events.

A few weeks later our commander told us we would remain interned during the rest of the war. Weighing anchor soon afterward, we steamed up to the Norfolk Navy Yard, where we came alongside our sister ship, the *Prinz Eitel Friedrich,* which had slipped in between the Capes precisely one month before us after a voyage of commerce raiding similar to our own. Here we cast anchor to give ourselves up to the protection and good will of the government of the United States.

Note. I stop the story at this point, for though the events of our internment were as interesting to me as those of the cruise itself, they do not properly belong to the history of the voyage.

INDEX OF SHIPS